"Hilary's compassionate heart for homem
tension of keeping a tidy home while tryin
spective shines through the pages of this
more importantly, the Scripture she weaves throughout this book—
will be a balm to every tired homemaker who has struggled with feeling like she just can't keep things tidy."

—**Erin Odom,** founder of The Humbled Homemaker® and author of
More Than Just Making It and *You Can Stay Home with Your Kids!*

"As Christian women, we dwell in an in-between land. On the one hand, we desire our home to be a place of rest and rejuvenation for our family, filled with peaceful and beautiful things. On the other hand, we can struggle with idolizing the perfect home and chasing after the Instagram-worthy house of our dreams that's just too far out of our budget. Hilary gets straight to the heart of this tightrope walk with relatable stories, biblical wisdom, and godly advice. Are you longing for a peaceful, tidy home? Hilary shares how to best accomplish this with true rest and beauty."

—**Jami Balmet,** creator of Finding Joy in Your Home and author of
the Finding Joy in Your Kitchen cookbook series

"As a homeschooling, work-from-home mom of three, I resonate with the struggle of wanting to keep a tidy house but always falling short. This book is a gift to all those like me. It holds out freedom and joy to women who've strived not only to have a tidy house but to present a tidy, perfect life to those around us. Hilary reminds us what truly matters in *The Tension of Tidy*."

—**Christie Thomas,** author of *Little Habits, Big Faith* and *Fruit Full*

"In the nitty-gritty of our everyday lives, *The Tension of Tidy* helps us recognize this difficult but undeniable truth: *Perfectionism equals grace rejection.* Through Scripture and story, Hilary serves as our candid-yet-kind guide to receiving and resting in God's comfort—in our homes, our hearts, and our relationships."

—**Cheri Gregory,** coauthor of *You Don't Have to Try So Hard* and *Overwhelmed*

"Most every woman deals daily with tension caused by the demands and expectations of home, work, family, and just living life! But warmly—with relatable anecdotes, practical inspiration, and biblical encouragement—Hilary Bernstein guides us to take all that tension we're so good at clenching and release it to our grace- and peace- and joy-giving heavenly Father."

—**JoAnne Simmons,** author of *The Overthinker's Devotional*

"The description of Hilary's college dorm room captured my attention, and I plunged in to read more about this burden-filled journey we call *perfection*. Her passion to direct women to the Lord and his written Word is evident, allowing her readers to recognize there is genuine freedom in Christ. The Tension Tamers in each chapter provide an opportunity for the practical application of truth to our hearts and lives."

—**Brenda McCord,** founder of Discover God's Truth Ministries and cohost of the *Walk with God* podcast

the tension of tidy

Uncovering God's Perfect Grace for Your Imperfect Space

Hilary Bernstein

FOREWORD BY ASHERITAH CIUCIU

KREGEL
PUBLICATIONS

The Tension of Tidy: Uncovering God's Perfect Grace for Your Imperfect Space
© 2025 by Hilary Bernstein

Published by Kregel Publications, a division of Kregel Inc., 2450 Oak Industrial Dr. NE, Grand Rapids, MI 49505. www.kregel.com.

Published in association with Books & Such Literary Management, www.booksandsuch.com.

The persons and events portrayed in this book have been used with permission. To protect the privacy of these individuals, some names and identifying details have been changed.

Cataloging-in-Publication Data is available from the Library of Congress.

ISBN 978-0-8254-4872-0, print
ISBN 978-0-8254-7441-5, epub
ISBN 978-0-8254-7440-8, Kindle

Printed in the United States of America
25 26 27 28 29 30 31 32 33 34 / 5 4 3 2 1

*For all my amazing sisters in Christ
who feel weighed down by
the pressure of perfection.*

Contents

Foreword

WHAT COMES TO mind when you hear the word *tidy*?

As a mom to three young kids, I immediately picture our living room floor—strewn with building blocks, books, dress-up clothes, and probably a few hidden candy wrappers too. Definitely the opposite of tidy.

To be fair, it's not just the kids. As I type these words, my husband is working to repair a plumbing leak that led to a massive hole in our kitchen ceiling. My desk is littered with Post-It notes, books, bills, and random papers to be filed. And I'm pretty sure there's a laundry basket of clean clothes upstairs just waiting to be folded and put away.

No matter how many cleaning systems we implement or how many "cleanup sprints" we attempt as a family, our home bears witness to the second law of thermodynamics—without constant intervention, our environment tends to devolve toward chaos and disorder.

It's easy to become envious when social media displays perfectly curated homes. It's easy to become resentful when others leave messes behind. It's easy to become snippy when we just want the stainless fridge to stay streak-free for more than an hour, thank-you-very-much.

But in those moments, I'm reminded that Jesus never asked me to keep a picture-perfect home. He does, however, invite me—and you—to abide in him, to receive his love, and to live out his love toward others, even in our imperfect spaces.

The Bible tells us that Jesus, the Son of God, left the realm of glory to come to this dusty, dirty, and disheveled world, to dwell among us—literally, to "pitch his tent" in our midst (see John 1:14–18). If ever there was someone entitled to complain about the conditions he was living in, it was Jesus. But he didn't. Instead, he entered imperfect spaces to welcome imperfect people to encounter his perfect loving presence.

And encountering Jesus changes everything, even how we tend our homes so that other people may encounter him there. That's why I'm grateful for the book you hold in your hands.

I've known Hilary for more than a decade now. We've dreamed of books together, we've watched our kids grow up together, and we've served in our local church together. We've been in each other's homes, both for sumptuous feasts and for simple cookouts. And when my family moved out of our newlywed home, Hilary's husband helped us paint over the sunshiny-yellow and berry-blue colors that would have never graced the pages of a magazine. But not once did I feel they judged us for our colorful walls or thrifted furniture.

So I can tell you: Hilary lives out what she teaches. She doesn't just offer quick tips for a cleaner home; she actually opens her life to share real stories of her own personal struggles in this area. And more importantly, she shares how God transformed her—and continues to grow her—in the areas of tidiness, hospitality, and a gracious heart.

In *The Tension of Tidy*, Hilary invites us to embrace the beauty of imperfection and discover God's grace in our messy, imperfect spaces. With a blend of warmth, relatability, and unwavering hope, she gently reminds us that our worth isn't measured by the cleanliness of our homes but by the love and grace of our heavenly Father.

So grab a cup of coffee or your favorite tea, and settle in. Let Hilary guide you as a dear friend, reminding you that in the tension of tidy, God's grace is ever-present.

I'm cheering you on as you invite God's creative Spirit to bring order and beauty to your chaos—inside and out.

With much joy,

Asheritah Ciuciu
Author of *Delighting in Jesus* and *Prayers of REST*

A Surprising Beginning

AN ODD ASSORTMENT of 1970s and '80s pop music from a local radio station blared from my bedside alarm clock, waking me from another night of sleep. After mentally singing along with the words, I hit the snooze button and rolled over, eyes wide open. It was morning, and I was fully aware I had more things to do today than the day had hours. I might have felt rested, but I did not want to get up.

My thoughts swirled around my circumstances. I had too much to do. I knew it, deep down. I listed the growing number of things I needed to get done at work today. I thought through the appointments I needed to make for my kids, and the important life lessons I should be teaching them. I couldn't forget to stop at the store to pick up the ingredients for a salad I promised to take to a potluck. I wondered when I'd fit in the time to visit my parents or take the dog to the vet.

After I hit the snooze button again, my mental to-do list for my family's home entered the picture. The kitchen floor looked filthy yesterday, and I needed to fit in some time to mop it. Mopping probably wouldn't be enough though—there were some spots that definitely needed some scrubbing on my hands and knees. That just couldn't happen today. Maybe tomorrow? Or this weekend? And my husband and I needed to talk about whether to call a plumber about the outdoor faucet, but I knew he was stressed over a work meeting. Would next week or next month be a better time to bring the topic up? It's not like we had the money set aside for that repair anyway.

My alarm went off again, and I finally climbed out of bed to start my day, even though I felt I had already lived it out in my imagination. This was becoming a daily occurrence, before I opened my Bible, poured myself a cup of coffee, hopped in the shower, made my bed, or even made it out of bed. Every morning I woke up thinking through the commitments, opportunities, and chores that lay ahead in my day and in my home. And every morning I got out of bed feeling defeated by all the tension.

When my friends and I got together in our spare time, we'd catch up about families and work and life, then we'd start to scratch the surface of how we felt about our homes. We were tired. Even though each of us were completely aware of every task that was necessary, we still felt unable to get started. No matter what we actually accomplished, it was never enough. Exhaustion, overwhelm, stress, and failure never went away. Sometimes we could block them out with the sheer amount of busyness in life, but they always found a way to resurface, like a mole that unfortunately and blindly scurries into a swimming pool during the night. (Is my family's pool the only place this happens? Each summer I'm familiar with this unfortunate demise, as I regularly end up as the mole scooper.)

Facing the Tension of Tidy

One day, as my literary agent Barb and I caught up about life and she asked how I was *really* doing, all the work pressures, family pressures, and home pressures that were building up inside came tumbling out in my words. I was struggling. And come to think of it, every single friend of mine was too.

Wisely, Barb challenged me that *this* was what I should write a book about: all the struggles women face in their homes every single day. I thought it was a fantastic idea for a book—for someone else to write.

At that moment, I wanted to *read* a book that would give me advice, encouragement, and biblical instruction. I wasn't so sure I wanted to remind myself about the homemaking defeat I lived in every day, pore over it some more, and then write about it. We ended our conversation with an agreement to pray about the idea.

Pray I did, asking God to give me insight and guidance in an area of life where I felt I was completely in over my head. The Lord did answer my prayers, and after I pondered this subject for a couple of weeks, I noticed that I lived with a lot more clarity and direction than I'd realized.

First of all, I recognized there are so many culprits behind the tensions we feel when it comes to our homes: our cultures, our families, our possessions, and ourselves, just to name a few. Whether we realize it or not, some of the tensions come from outside sources that we can't control. Other tensions, internal ones, run much deeper. While the pressures and influences that come from external sources are strong and can intensify when we least expect them to, sometimes those internal expectations and stressors are infinitely worse. Unfortunately, we are often our own worst enemies.

Sometimes the tensions themselves don't seem that intense, at least from the outside looking in. What *is* intense are the ways we internalize and amplify certain issues until they overwhelm us. So many external pressures from the world and internal tensions from ourselves have uncanny ways of pushing us toward feelings of failure and discouragement. Instead of recognizing and celebrating the wins that happen in our homes, we're left mentally bullying ourselves, thinking we need to do more and be more.

All the tension can feel like a taut rope wrapping around us, making it hard to move or even breathe. But there's a way to cut this stranglehold and free ourselves. That freedom can be found in the sword of the Spirit, better known as the Word of God. God directed me to truths in the Bible—especially in the Psalms—that are just as timely and effective right now as when they were first written thousands of years ago. I recognized that they could help us deal with our universal feelings of frustration and exhaustion.

Once I identified the main tensions when it comes to homemaking, as well as relevant scriptural principles, I thought through my years of trial and error in my home. All my mistakes and victories had helped me figure out practical ways to manage my home in the middle of the unpredictability of life. I knew what boosted my confidence and motivated me. I was familiar with what worked well and what fizzled miserably.

Throughout this entire time of praying and pondering, I experienced the beauty and peace of God's grace as he gently reminded me that my worth wasn't found in what my home looked like or how much I could or could not accomplish. And that, dear reader, is how *The Tension of Tidy* began.

Meeting the Founder of Homes

Really, though, *The Tension of Tidy* has its true origin all the way back at the beginning of the Bible. You see, there we learn why we care so much about our homes, as well as the reason why caring for them is filled with so much tension.

God created the earth and everything in it, including the first man and woman. He created a home for them as well, and it was good. As Genesis 2:7–9 recounts,

> Then the LORD God formed the man of dust from the ground and breathed into his nostrils the breath of life, and the man became a living creature. And the LORD God planted a garden in Eden, in the east, and there he put the man whom he had formed. And out of the ground the LORD God made to spring up every tree that is pleasant to the sight and good for food.

Before he created Eve, the woman, the Lord planted a garden and

put the man, Adam, there to live. And how did he furnish this garden? With every tree that was "pleasant to the sight and good for food."
Imagine a lush, beautiful garden laden with food—that sounds a lot
like a well-stocked kitchen in a home. After that, the Lord saw that it
wasn't good for man to be alone (see verse 18), so he took the man's rib
and formed a woman (see verses 21–22). That woman was created in
the garden home. She became the man's companion and helped him
care for their perfect home.

Unfortunately, as you and I know from the minute-to-minute tensions we face, the world didn't stay perfect. Humanity's flawless beginning took a tragic turn—the man and woman believed Satan's lies
and disobeyed God (see 3:1–7). Part of the punishment and curse their
sin brought into the world was the new reality that their home would
no longer be a perfect space:

> Cursed is the ground because of you;
> With hard labor you shall eat from it
> All the days of your life.
> Both thorns and thistles it shall grow for you;
> Yet you shall eat the plants of the field;
> By the sweat of your face
> You shall eat bread,
> Until you return to the ground,
> Because from it you were taken;
> For you are dust,
> And to dust you shall return.
>
> (verses 17–19 NASB)

This is why you and I both live every single day in a world—and
in homes—filled with troubles and toil. It's the reason I start my days
trying to figure out how to squeeze in all I'm convinced I need to do.
It's the reason we try so hard to jump through hoop after hoop in our

homes, spurred on by unintentional and intentional pressures from so many sources. Stop for a moment and imagine: What would your life and home and job look and feel like today if nothing on earth had ever fallen from the very good condition that God created them in?

Although we can never go back to Eden and the perfect home and life we lost, the good news is there is something promising ahead of us. Just like the Bible begins with a picture of dwelling in a perfect home, it ends with this picture too. At the end of the Bible, in Revelation 21:1–4, we're given a hint of what this future, forever home will be like:

> Then I saw a new heaven and a new earth, for the first heaven and the first earth had passed away, and the sea was no more. And I saw the holy city, new Jerusalem, coming down out of heaven from God, prepared as a bride adorned for her husband. And I heard a loud voice from the throne saying, "Behold, the dwelling place of God is with man. He will dwell with them, and they will be his people, and God himself will be with them as their God. He will wipe away every tear from their eyes, and death shall be no more, neither shall there be mourning, nor crying, nor pain anymore, for the former things have passed away."

Aside from being beautifully adorned, this forever home centers on who will dwell there: God. He will dwell with his people. Just like Adam and Eve weren't alone in the garden, we won't be alone in our new home. God himself will dwell with us!

Did you notice what *won't* be there? No more crying, dying, or pain. No more sin. No more tension. They will all pass away.

Soaking in God's Perfect Grace

Scripture's principles are much more promising and helpful than popular, pithy sayings we're inundated with daily. For every catchy phrase that encourages us to do more, be more, work harder, or make things happen in our own strength, the Bible is brimming with grace-filled reminders. Instead of making us feel like we need to wear ourselves out trying harder, God's truth ministers to us in our deepest parts. It gets to the root of things. It speaks to our hearts. Throughout this book, we'll dive into the Bible for truth that can comfort us and set us free from the intense tensions we feel as we attempt to care for our homes. As I share stories and tips that work for me and my family, I'll also offer Tension Tamers along the way—reflection questions, practical advice, and helpful challenges.

Just like with our homes, sometimes you need to make a mess before things can get cleaner. Some tensions, like certain rooms in our homes, might seem messier than others, but by the end of this journey together, we'll experience freedom that only comes from the Lord. As we turn to the truth of God's Word and begin to internalize and live out his timeless principles, we'll uncover his perfect grace for our imperfect spaces.

Chapter 1

Perfection

PERFECT. AFTER ARRANGING a throw pillow just so and adjusting the area rug in a particular way, my dorm room looked flawless. Everything was in its proper place.

I labored for this sort of perfection as a college student in a teensy, tiny dorm room, of all places. Instead of spending all my free time hanging out with friends or watching TV or studying a little harder, I made sure my room was immaculate.

Fast-forward twenty-five years, and I was living the life I only dreamed about back in college—married with children and a dog, coming home to a cozy bungalow in a cutesy neighborhood—but my house was far from perfect.

To be clear, most of my house was in pretty good shape. If you walked through my front door at any time and inspected my living room, dining room, kitchen, and bathroom, you probably would have considered my home to be very tidy. And if my younger college-student self could have seen it, she would have had to admit that although it wasn't as spotless as her dorm room, it was still surprisingly clean considering an actual busy family lived in it.

But shut away behind closed doors in my basement, there was a

disastrous wreck. A lot like Monica in *Friends* with her horribly cluttered closet, I didn't let people into this space of towering stuff. I even
avoided going there myself, unless I absolutely had to. I had a vague
idea of where things might be stored, but I didn't want to set aside
a huge chunk of time to go find something in that room. And the
thought of a purging process? It was overwhelming. I doubted I'd ever
have enough time to tackle that disaster, so I dealt with it the only way
I could think of: I shut the door. Out of sight, out of mind, right?

Only the situation felt more like out of sight, *heavy* on my mind. I
imagined that if I unexpectedly died in my sleep, my husband, kids,
parents, and friends would be stuck dealing with that oppressive storage space, asking themselves when was the last time I had listened to
my cassette tapes from the nineties or wondering why in the world I
owned so many different cookie cutters if I only baked cutout cookies
at Christmas.

I might've only walked into that mess of a storage room a couple of
times a week, but I always had it on my mind. And that mess made me
feel awful. No matter how clean I tried to keep the rest of my house
or how hard I worked to get to the dishes and laundry each day, I still
felt the suffocating weight of that imperfection. Instead of celebrating
the fact that I managed to keep the livable part of my home relatively
clean, even with kids and pets, I couldn't ever shake the nagging feeling that my house wasn't clean, just because of that one room.

As much as I wanted that basement room cleaned—a desire fueled
by my drive for perfection—I also only had so much time and energy
each day. And I never seemed to have enough to tackle that storage
space. (In recent years, God has helped me deal with the clutter of that
room in some unexpected ways. Now it's much less of a burden, but I'll
share more of that story in upcoming chapters.)

Even though I fully grasp how limited my time is and how fleeting
my energy is, part of me still wants every single nook and cranny of my
home, basement, and garage to be spotless and organized. That's utterly

ridiculous! And yet, as a woman *without* obsessive-compulsive disorder, I continually wrestle with this picture of perfection for my home. I feel deflated when all the spaces and places in my home are *not* perfect like my teensy college dorm room used to be. I often ponder how I can better manage this delicate balance of caring for my home and living the life the Lord's given me—without feeling defeated day after day.

The tension of perfection comes when we grasp the truth that our time, energy, and funds have realistic limits, yet we still find ourselves drawn to the fallacy that we need to keep homes that are fit to grace the pages of a magazine or feature on a home improvement show. The tension gets even worse when we saddle ourselves with guilt whenever we can't meet our ideal expectations or live up to society's impossible standard of perfect homes that are beautifully decorated and immaculately maintained.

You may enjoy cleaning and prefer a tidy home. Or maybe messiness is part of who you are. Regardless of your preferred tendency for tidiness, we all face pressure when it comes to caring for our homes. Where do these invisible, impossible standards come from? And how do we break free?

Embracing the Goodness of Work

Every homemaker knows a home doesn't take care of itself—not even a perfect one. There is always work to be done to manage and maintain our belongings. As much as we may wish it were otherwise, it has been like this since the beginning. Let's take a closer look at the story of creation in Genesis.

The original bachelor pad, the comfortable haven of Eden was not just something for man to enjoy—he was also responsible for tending it. Genesis 2:15 reveals, "The Lord God took the man and put him in the garden of Eden to work it and keep it." Before there was sin and before there was a curse, man was set in this beautiful, fruitful garden and charged with caring for it.

Just like today's gardens require a lot of time, attention, and hard work, the first garden would've required much effort. Imagine what pre-fall, pre-flood gardening might have included! Most likely this first gardener would've tended to the soil, nurtured seedlings, pruned plants, and harvested fruit. Even without the constant annoyances of weeds and destructive pests, drought, or flooding, he still would've needed to tend to many continual garden chores.

When God saw that it wasn't good for man to be alone, he made woman and she joined the man in the work of caring for their garden home. And that wasn't all they were responsible for:

> Then God said, "Let Us make mankind in Our image, accord-
> ing to Our likeness; and let them rule over the fish of the sea
> and over the birds of the sky and over the livestock and over
> all the earth, and over every crawling thing that crawls on the
> earth." So God created man in His own image, in the image
> of God He created him; male and female He created them.
> (1:26–27 NASB)

From the beginning, it's clear that work was an essential part of God's original plan for humanity. How do we know this? Genesis 1:31 explains, "God saw everything that he had made"—that includes humanity's assignments to keep the garden and rule over the earth—"and behold, it was very good."

Amazingly, even in perfect Eden, there was work to be done—and that was good!

Acknowledging the Tension of Homemaking

Although homes—and the work of caring for them—were part of God's perfectly created world, we all are painfully aware that we don't live in that unfallen world of perfection. Our earthly lives will always be stuck between the first, perfect home God made for humans that's described in Genesis and the second, perfect home he promises in Revelation to those who believe in Christ. We're surrounded by imperfection everywhere we look, and our lives, homes, relationships, and work all are caught in a relentless tug-of-war battle between the good they were created to be and the broken versions that sin has created.

On the one hand, we realize that homes are good. They're a part of God's purpose and plan, and we can appreciate them and thank God for his good gifts. Making our homes into lovely havens of rest and relaxation can be very good. After all, God is the Master Artist. He created beauty, and he created humans to have an eye for it. Our desires to surround ourselves with beautiful things can be good as long as they glorify God and fill us with gratitude.

On the other hand, once we cross over to obsessing about—or dare I say idolizing—the homes of our dreams, we've gone too far. When we notice our quest for beautiful things in our homes has started stealing our joy or adoration for God, that's a sign we need to dial things back.

Just as fixating on our furnishings and finishing touches elevates our homes to positions they were never meant to hold in our minds, obsessing over the cleanliness of our homes creates a false aspiration of flawlessness.

Many of us, whether we realize it or not, seek validation of our worth in how we keep our homes. We believe that if the places where we live look or feel perfect, we must be doing our proper duty. Yet there's absolutely nothing biblical about this perspective. Contrary to popular belief, we'll never find the phrase "Cleanliness is next to godliness" anywhere in the Bible. It's simply a trite saying someone made up and a lot of people like to quote. Still, many homemakers wrestle with unrealistic expectations of perfectly tidy homes and believe that the cleanliness of our homes somehow reflects our worth or even our holiness.

I can assure you that a godly life has absolutely nothing to do with the state of your home.

Yes, God is a God of order, as 1 Corinthians 14:33 (NIV) reveals. And if we're good stewards of the many gifts he's entrusted to us (see 1 Peter 4:10), we will faithfully care for our homes. But our righteousness does not depend on our cleaning habits.

Whether we succeed or fail in meeting the standards we establish in our own minds of what a perfect home is, we need to remember that the pressures and expectations don't define us. Judging and bullying ourselves with self-defeat and self-loathing isn't healthy, and it isn't biblical. The apostle Paul called believers to "work willingly at whatever you do, as though you were working for the Lord rather than for people. Remember . . . the Master you are serving is Christ" (Colossians 3:23–24 NLT). But working for the Lord doesn't mean you put yourself down or work yourself to the point of exhaustion day after day, week after week.

We also need to understand that working as though it's for the *Lord* isn't the same as working for amazing *stuff*. Are you adding stress to your workload just because you're trying to buy or maintain certain belongings? Is your quest for a room that looks exactly like something you saw on TV stealing your rest and peace of mind?

In fact, seeking perfection in our homes ends up being a cheap replacement for the Lord. A substitute picture of perfection has been drilled into our subconscious our entire lives: a flawlessness that we've internalized from our modern, materialistic culture. We've been discipled by our society to find our identity and satisfaction in our belongings and homes, yet those material belongings keep us far from our true identity and source of satisfaction: our Savior. If we notice that we're completely trusting in ourselves to make things happen around our homes—trusting in our own inspiration, or the money we're spending on renovations, or how good our homes make us feel— it's time to take a breather and get a fresh perspective.

Enjoying the Gift of Dwelling Places

While the Bible ends with a picture of God dwelling with humans in the book of Revelation, descriptions and promises of dwelling with him now are sprinkled throughout the Bible, particularly in the Psalms. As poetic prayers set smack-dab in the middle of the Bible, the psalms are songs of joy and grief, pleasure and pain. Just as the psalms teach us how we can safely express our emotions in God's presence, their timeless wisdom also helps us gather an accurate, biblical perspective on our imperfect homes.

Over and over, we can read the Psalms and learn about what it means to dwell *in* the Lord and *with* the Lord. As we dwell with him here and now, we can experience his perfect grace and peace that's so refreshing and restful compared with the tensions we face.

Before we consider the details of dwelling with the Lord, though, what exactly does it mean to *dwell*? Several Hebrew words are translated in our English Bibles as "dwell." They carry the meanings of remaining, abiding, settling down, residing, staying, and inhabiting. Consider this residing, settling down, and abiding when you read Bible verses like what Moses shared in Psalm 90:1: "Lord, you have been our dwelling place in all generations," or the words of Psalm 91:1: "Whoever dwells in the shelter of the Most High will rest in the shadow of the Almighty" (NIV). As we dwell with our heavenly Father here in our earthly lives, we can remain in his house (see 27:4), ever singing his praise (see 84:4) and abiding in his presence (see 140:13).

We can soak in and appreciate this opportunity to dwell, remain, or stay in a relationship with the Lord as we live this temporary, earthly life and anticipate a permanent, eternal life that's yet to come. Just like he created homes on earth in the first place, our heavenly Father also established a plan so that those who believe in his Son will one day dwell in his heavenly home. Right now, though, we can also recognize the blessing of what it means to dwell in actual, physical homes. Here on earth, God intends for people to dwell in homes so we're not left as wandering vagabonds. Our homes are merciful gifts from him.

Building Our Homes

One of the first passages that opened my eyes to the homemaking wisdom for our actual, physical homes was Psalm 127:1–2:

> Unless the LORD builds the house,
>   those who build it labor in vain.
> Unless the LORD watches over the city,
>   the watchman stays awake in vain.
> It is in vain that you rise up early
>   and go late to rest,
> eating the bread of anxious toil;
>   for he gives to his beloved sleep.

As we dig into these two verses, let's consider the first three words of this psalm: _Unless the Lord._ We need to know that _unless the Lord_ does the work, our attempts will be empty, without purpose, and useless. When we leave the Lord out of the picture and try to build our homes with only our own energy, expertise, and strength, our efforts will lack so much. Unless the Lord is doing a good work in your home, housework and chores can make you feel like you're suffering through an endless uphill battle.

It's a striking conditional statement: Unless the Lord is actively involved, you won't get the results you'd like. Unless he builds your house, you'll work and work and work without a preferable outcome.

Keep in mind that this psalm was written by Solomon, someone who personally experienced the Lord's way of building a house. The book of 1 Kings includes an account of Solomon's twenty-year building process for both his palace and the Lord's temple (see chapters

6–10). The stones were prepared at a quarry. Wood covered the interior so no stones were seen. Then the inside of the house of the Lord was overlaid with pure gold. And through the Lord's blessing, world rulers sent Solomon riches and treasures like gold and precious stones. First Kings 10:23–25 tells us:

> King Solomon excelled all the kings of the earth in riches and in wisdom. And the whole earth sought the presence of Solomon to hear his wisdom, which God had put into his mind. Every one of them brought his present, articles of silver and gold, garments, myrrh, spices, horses, and mules, so much year by year.

Only the Lord could have lavished so many blessings on the spectacular building project. As a result of seeing this extravagant provision throughout his life and his kingly reign, Solomon was able to attest that unless the Lord had been building his house, those who constructed it would've labored in vain. On his own, Solomon would've labored in vain.

If the Lord is the one who's central to our work, does that mean we have permission to be lazy? Do we have an excuse to stop trying and expect the Lord to do everything? Of course not. The God of the universe is not a magician or a mystical butler who will instantly make the work around our homes disappear. We shouldn't come to him with a hope or expectation for *Abracadabra! Shazam!* All your housework mysteriously completed in an instant!

Our homes will not be cleaned as effortlessly as pulling a rabbit out of a hat. We must still do the work. And, most likely, the work will be hard. But that hard work is biblical. As Psalm 128:2 tells us, "You shall eat the fruit of the labor of your hands; you shall be blessed, and it shall be well with you." There's no getting around it—the "labor of your hands" will be laborious.

Yes, hard work is essential, both in everyday life and in your home. But *trusting* in your own efforts and hard work will sabotage the way you can invite the Lord to build, establish, and do his good work. As Lydia Brownback explains in her book *Sing a New Song*, "Depending on God is no call to passivity; to the contrary, the wisdom of Solomon calls us to be proactive in living out our callings and performing our daily tasks. So the work is ours; however, the success of our work is not. The outcome of all we do lies completely in the hands of God."[1]

What is useless, empty, and vain? Laboring *without* the Lord. Waking up at the crack of dawn to get ahead with tasks and chores or staying up late at night working and working around your home out of fear and distrust, believing that it's all up to you.

Tension Tamer

Think about the frustration you feel when you consider different chores or aspects around your home. Are you trying to solve these problems with your own resourcefulness, a clever tip you discovered online, or new strategies you heard about on a podcast? Or are you asking the Lord to step in? Is the Lord building your home?

Laboring with the Lord

Like changing gears in a car, the shift from trying to build my home in my strength to surrendering things to the Lord is evident. When I attempt things on my own, I feel like the entire weight of my home sits on my shoulders. I don't have enough time in my day to get everything done. My chores drain my energy, my kids need whatever time I could've used for catching up on housework, and routines seem to fly out the window.

But when I stop to pray and ask the Lord to multiply my time and energy? Things get done. Not everything on my to-do list gets completed, because he brings people and situations into my day in unexpected, beautiful ways. But I can see progress in my home and family without so much struggle. My heart is at peace, routines go smoothly, and my focus often shifts from tasks to people. Instead of ending the day feeling overwhelmed and behind, I feel like I actually accomplished something.

The liberating news for you and me is that we don't have to make things happen. We don't have to overwork ourselves and wear ourselves out. Trying to do it all in our own power is empty and useless. Instead, we can work diligently and then rest, noticing what the Lord accomplishes through us and for us. We can slow down and enjoy the basic luxuries of life—like eating and sleeping. After all, they're good gifts from God.

As the Lord builds our homes, the tension from perfection washes away in his perfect peace.

Our willing surrender means we choose to take our burdens and heave them onto Jesus. Just like Psalm 55:22 shares,

> Cast your burden on the LORD,
>   and he will sustain you;
> he will never permit
>   the righteous to be moved.

Jesus himself directs in Matthew 11:28, "Come to me, all you who are weary and burdened, and I will give you rest" (NIV). He gives rest and relief. We simply need to come to him.

If we're being honest, rest and relief aren't always associated with our homes or our hearts, are they? Instead, we think of the things we want or need to do. We concentrate on unfinished to-do lists and the routines we think we need for our particular seasons of life. Then we try to rush and rearrange, deceived by the fantasy that if we can just figure out a way to balance everything, our homes and lives will look and feel perfect.

This world may dupe us into thinking that finding balance is the key to life. But consider that concept. Balance means we need to evenly distribute the elements in our lives to achieve equilibrium. Any adult woman knows this is virtually impossible in real life! If you consider the demands thrown on you by your family, job, other relationships, and then add your home to the equation, everything falls blatantly off-balance. Any kind of equilibrium feels impossible.

When I think about the responsibilities and tasks required for my job, I'm faced with a seemingly never-ending to-do list. I can work as hard as possible every day, but I'll never get completely caught up. The same goes with my responsibilities and chores at home. Just when I think my house is clean and I'm caught up with laundry and dishes, someone makes a meal or changes their clothing, and my work cycle begins all over again. Adding my husband and children to the picture only drives home the fact that I'm never finished pouring into them and investing in our relationships.

If I focus on these continual demands, pressure begins to build and I start to tense up, feeling the strain of not being able to complete everything. But isn't this self-inflicted stress just a reminder of who I'm trusting in?

When we only consider what *we* can personally do, we focus on ourselves and our strength. We remove God from the equation and zero in on our shortcomings. We don't have enough time or energy or patience or ability to do everything. And what does Psalm 127:1 reveal? "Unless the LORD builds the house, those who build it labor in vain." All that anxious toil of ours is completely in vain.

Instead of concentrating on what we know we can't do, we need to prayerfully take those feelings to the Lord. God can do what he needs to do. Unless *he* builds our marriages, then our humble, flawed efforts can only go so far. Unless *he* builds our parenting, we will fail. Unless *he's* the one who builds our careers or ministries, the work we attempt is in vain. And unless *he* builds our homes and multiplies our time, energy, and ideas so we can care for them day by day, we'll drown in overwhelm all the time. It's amazing to experience the freedom that comes from trusting the Lord to build something worthwhile in our homes. We still have work to do, but it's *his* work to do. Instead of considering how to work out *our* solutions, we get to work out *his* solutions and watch how he works everything together.

Giving God All the Pieces

When my kids were young, my parents treated my family to a week at the beach each summer. And every time, the adults would spend our late nights working on large jigsaw puzzles after the kids were tucked into bed. One year, we started building our puzzle by finding all the corners and edges, but we quickly discovered that our puzzle pieces didn't match the picture on the box.

After the initial anger and frustration wore off—how dare the manufacturer put the wrong pieces in the box!—we kept working on the puzzle. Working only from the colors and shapes was much more difficult than we would've chosen, but by the end of the week we fit the final pieces together and saw our masterpiece.

Our puzzle looked nothing like we initially anticipated, and the process was longer, more draining, and more frustrating than we'd hoped, but the finished product was complete. And that puzzle was beautiful.

In much the same way, what God has in mind for our lives and homes and families may look completely different from anything we imagine. Isaiah 55:8 reminds us, "For my thoughts are not your thoughts, neither are your ways my ways, declares the LORD." We may feel pressured into thinking the finished product of our lives and homes should turn out one way, but he surprises us with puzzle pieces that are unlike anything we could've asked for or expected.

If we faithfully keep working with what he's given us in our homes, we'll realize that the beauty in his design is more perfect than anything we could have planned on our own. As we remember that his ways are better than ours, we'll begin to break free from the suffocating squeeze of perfection's viselike grip. We'll experience true freedom in our hearts and in our homes as we're liberated from the tension of perfection.

Chapter 2

The Quest for More

I COME FROM a family of collectors. Not of treasures like fine art or extravagant jewelry or vintage cars, or even rare accumulations like the world's largest collection of Dutch salt and pepper shakers. No, my mom, aunts, and grandmas collected things they enjoyed. Whether it was my mom's snowmen decorations, my aunt's snow globes, or my grandma's duck decoys, these collections would grow larger and larger every year as birthday gifts added to their number.

This habit of collecting was passed down to me. When I was a teen, I was encouraged to choose what I wanted to collect. What would be the one special theme of items I'd want to display in my home someday? Once I considered and tried quite a few collections, I finally embraced collecting blown glass Christmas ornaments.

While collectible items make thoughtful gifts and fun souvenirs, there comes a point when a person owns enough of a certain thing. For my own collection, I appreciate the memories tied to each ornament, but I'm out of room on my Christmas trees. I don't need more ornaments. My mom doesn't need more snowmen either.

But even when we have plenty, the quest for more calls to us, doesn't it? Maybe we aren't drawn to collectibles, but we want a bigger house or better furniture or the latest kitchen gadget or something more in our homes. The desire to accumulate more and more is sometimes insatiable. Why do we always want to keep changing and adding to what we already have?

Avoiding the Comparison Trap

I grew up in the pre-digital age when we found fashion or home inspiration in monthly magazines, we read the news once a day in the newspaper, and every night after the late-night news and talk shows, television stations went off the air. That meant every station stopped broadcasting until the morning—the national anthem would play with an image of the American flag, then television screens would either go blank or staticky. People communicated with each other through letters, at face-to-face gatherings, and over phone conversations. Because most telephones had cords, when we were ready to make a phone call, we were tethered to one spot until that conversation ended. (Stuck on the phone with someone who had the gift of gab? Hopefully the phone had an extra-long cord or a comfy seat nearby.) In this kind of environment of limitations, there was no onslaught of noise and news at all hours of the day and night, no constant crush of communication.

Our information age is changing us, for sure, but not necessarily for the better.

We're faced daily with nonstop comparison traps, but even though they've become incessant in the digital age, they've been around forever. Comparison has existed since Eve and Adam gave in to temptation and sin entered the world. Didn't Eve compare what God gave her with what the serpent offered? And what was one of the issues her son Cain struggled with? Comparing himself with his brother Abel.

This comparison tendency is what the Sons of Korah, creators of eleven psalms, addressed in Psalm 49:16–19 (NASB):

Do not be afraid when a person becomes rich,
When the splendor of his house is increased;
For when he dies, he will take nothing with him;
His wealth will not descend after him.
Though while he lives he congratulates himself—
And though people praise you when you do well for yourself—
He will go to the generation of his fathers;
They will never see the light.

Throughout history, people have been fascinated by the lifestyles of the rich and famous and compared the ultrawealthy with their ordinary ways of life. While it may not be healthy or right—in 1 Timothy 6:9, Paul warned, "But those who desire to be rich fall into temptation, into a snare, into many senseless and harmful desires that plunge people into ruin and destruction"—comparing what you have with what someone else has is part of human nature.

Comparison is only encouraged by our current culture. For example, home improvement programs do a fantastic job entertaining us with show after show that leaves us wanting more from our homes. Popular programs fixate on what is annoying or just plain ugly about houses, but then the homeowners discover satisfaction and pleasure when they create the showplace of their dreams with the help of a whole lot of money and the right designers and contractors.

But there are plenty of problems with these comparison traps. For one, when we begin comparing ourselves with someone else, we simply don't know the entire story of that other person's life. We can't be sure how hard she worked for her home or if she didn't work at all. We don't know the positive or negative situations and circumstances in her life that enabled her to make certain purchases. We don't know the stress or lack of stress that accompanies her lifestyle. Since we're not mind readers and we don't have the inside scoop, we have no way of knowing her struggles or how her reality might be imperfect.

Not having a full picture is one problem, but there's an even bigger issue with comparison: When we wish we could magically trade places with someone else, we buy into the lie that God has somehow made a mistake in our own lives. The same liar that tempted Eve whispers to us, "Why does your life need to be the way God made it when you could have so much more?"

But here's the truth: God doesn't make mistakes. If our lives are what the Lord has planned for each of us, and if he's truly the one building our lives, why do we feel like *our* plans would be better than his? Philippians 4:19 promises, "My God will supply every need of yours according to his riches in glory in Christ Jesus." If we believe God's Word is true, let's stop doubting his faithful, amazing provision. If he "will supply every need of yours according to his riches in glory," isn't that more than enough (Philippians 4:19)? Aren't his riches far better than anything on this earth?

Storing Up Treasures

Not only do earthly riches fail to guarantee happiness or contentment, they also won't last forever, no matter what we may hope. In Psalm 49:10–12 (NLT), the Sons of Korah remind us:

> Those who are wise must finally die,
>   just like the foolish and senseless,
>   leaving all their wealth behind.
> The grave is their eternal home,
>   where they will stay forever.
> They may name their estates after themselves,
>   but their fame will not last.
> They will die, just like animals.

The young and the old, the rich and the poor, the wise and the fool all think about the here and now. In the midst of typical day-to-day life, it's easy to get wrapped up in what we can see and feel. And it can be difficult to remember that tomorrow is never guaranteed. You and I can be so prone to focusing on details like figuring out what's for dinner tomorrow night or creating inspiration boards before we pick a new sofa. But decisions and desires that seem so important to us in the moment may quickly disappear.

From ancient times to now, part of the human experience is that we build our wealth and fame and we personalize our homes in such detailed ways that they seem more like estates. We spend so much of our time, effort, and thought into building up what will never last. Yet David prayed from a different perspective in Psalm 39:4–7 (NLT):

> "LORD, remind me how brief my time on earth will be.
>> Remind me that my days are numbered—
>> how fleeting my life is.
> You have made my life no longer than the width of my hand.
>> My entire lifetime is just a moment to you;
>> at best, each of us is but a breath."
>
> We are merely moving shadows,
>> and all our busy rushing ends in nothing.
> We heap up wealth,
>> not knowing who will spend it.
> And so, Lord, where do I put my hope?
>> My only hope is in you.

Psalms 39 and 49 both offer the same sobering reminder: Everyone dies. Everyone leaves their wealth behind. And even if we work hard to heap it up during our time here on earth, we have very little idea or control about what will happen to our money or possessions once we're dead.

As various family members have passed away, I have come to fully grasp the reality of our personal collections. Someday each of us will die, and when we're gone, no one will care about our treasured collections like we did. In fact, most likely they'll end up on the shelves of the local resale shop just like so many I've walked past. Sometimes I take my time to appreciate the wide variety of bells or decorative spoons a person amassed. In the case of collectible clowns, I walk by in a hurry. Yet I wonder how resale shoppers will react to my glass Christmas ornament collection?

Collections aren't bad. I know the thrill of hunting and finally finding a specific treasured piece. Seeing particular collectibles and recalling vivid memories is wonderful. So if you happen to be a collector, enjoy your collections. But we need to keep a sober view in mind that someday our collections won't be our own. And they may not be as special as we'd like to think.

This is true for any material possession that we quest for more of. The time and money we spend acquiring and caring for these items might be better used somewhere else. After all, Jesus taught, "Sell your possessions and give to those in need. This will store up treasure for you in heaven! And the purses of heaven never get old or develop holes. Your treasure will be safe; no thief can steal it and no moth can destroy it. Wherever your treasure is, there the desires of your heart will also be" (Luke 12:33–34 NLT). As we remember this, we might be able to quench our desire for more.

Investing in Our Forever Home

We may feel like we're living with a healthy view of reality and know that life on this earth won't last forever. Yet we still might find ourselves investing so much of our time, energy, and money into our homes and possessions. When seeking the latest and greatest home improvement just to create a swoonworthy home starts adding tension to our lives, it's time to slow down and check our motives. Are we questing for more because we truly need the biggest or best kitchens? Why do we feel tempted to pour a lot of thought and money into a home improvement project even though the changes will end up being outdated in a decade? Currently, the trends in home colors are radically switching from one year to the next, making it nearly impossible to keep up with the latest fads unless we invest a lot of time, attention, and money into an ongoing popularity contest.

Please don't get me wrong: I'm not against home improvements! In my family's current seventy-five-year-old home, my husband and I are updating many features of our house and yard so the property is more livable. We're fixing serious problems that need to be addressed, like replacing our leaky roof and waterproofing a basement that flooded in the past. When we finally got tired of cooking off the two working burners on our ancient kitchen cooktop, we were excited to replace the old with new. But our reason for upgrading our appliance was because we cook a lot and two burners just weren't cutting it, not because we wanted our kitchen to somehow become a showplace that could last forever. As nice as the shiny new kitchen appliance was, the thrill was gone after a week or two. I fully realize that one day our nice stovetop will become old and outdated.

For those of us who seek security, peace, and confirmation of our worth in our homes, what will happen when we discover how fleeting those places really are? What about when we realize we're always wanting something more that seems just out of reach? What's left when we realize that stuff is just stuff?

While there's nothing inherently wrong with making renovations, especially if something truly needs improvement, we need to keep in mind that none of these improvements will last. One day our homes will crumble and fall. Things will break or rust or leak. Dents and dings will appear, and dust and dirt will accumulate.

Our homes aren't the only things that eventually fall apart. Every person, no matter how hard he or she tries, will die and leave their possessions and homes to someone else. As King David wisely observed in Psalm 39:6,

> Surely a man goes about as a shadow!
> Surely for nothing they are in turmoil;
>   man heaps up wealth and does not know who will gather!

Earth is temporary. We're strangers and aliens here, waiting for our eternal home. We try so hard to invest our hearts, souls, finances, and time into the equivalents of temporary hotel rooms while we're on our way to an infinitely better, permanent destination. We're just passing through, but we mislead ourselves into thinking we're permanent residents who need to improve our short-term rental properties.

Paul addressed this tension between the temporal and eternal in 2 Corinthians 4:16–5:4 when he wrote,

> We do not lose heart. Though our outer self is wasting away, our inner self is being renewed day by day. For this light momentary affliction is preparing for us an eternal weight of glory beyond all comparison, as we look not to the things that are seen but to the things that are unseen. For the things that are seen are transient, but the things that are unseen are eternal.
>
> For we know that if the tent that is our earthly home is destroyed, we have a building from God, a house not made with hands, eternal in the heavens. For in this tent we groan, longing to put on our heavenly dwelling, if indeed by putting it on we may not be found naked. For while we are still in this tent, we groan, being burdened—not that we would be unclothed, but that we would be further clothed, so that what is mortal may be swallowed up by life.

This temporal versus eternal tension is something all believers in Christ feel. While we're here on this earth in our mortal bodies, we groan and are burdened. It might feel tempting to lose heart, especially when it's evident that life in these short-term rental properties is hard. But Paul gave us the solution in 2 Corinthians 5:6–9: "We are always of good courage. We know that while we are at home in the body we are away from the Lord, for we walk by faith, not by sight. Yes, we are of good courage, and we would rather be away from the body and at home with the Lord. So whether we are at home or away, we make it our aim to please him."

Did you catch that? Whether we're in our short-term rentals on earth or in our forever, eternal home, we try to please the Lord. And we fix our eyes not on what is seen here and now, but on what is unseen.

Tension Tamer

What are you questing after? Stop and consider why. Since your time on earth is temporary, why do you invest so much in your physical home? Are you elevating your home and giving it eternal value when it's a passing fancy that will one day fade away?

Practically speaking, what in the world does having an eternal perspective mean for the way we care for our homes? If you happen to have an all-or-nothing tendency like me, it can be tempting to think that we should step back and stop caring about our homes if they're so temporary. However, every night I've stayed in a hotel, I've taken care of the room by picking up after myself, and I haven't slammed doors or wrecked the furniture. The same is true for all the apartments I've ever rented. I didn't own them, and I didn't intend on staying in them for a long time, but I still took care of them like they were my own. In the same way, as we go about our lives, we can care for and even invest in the homes God has given us, while still realizing and remembering they're temporary.

Escaping from Picture-Perfect Propaganda

Even when we realize our earthly homes won't last forever, we often try to live like they will. Part of this is cultivated by the daily onslaught of ads enticing us to buy more, more, more.

Home improvement shows aren't the only culprits of stirring discontentment with what we have and leading us down a path of constant comparing and upgrading. Promotional emails aren't the only sources that tempt us to buy more. Retailers keep cranking out gorgeous merchandise, and the push to buy comes in the form of commercials and ads consumed every single day.

Sometimes we don't even need advertising to convince us that we should buy something else. The home section of any store is easily one of my favorite places to browse because I always find plenty of attractive new options that would look nice in my home. If I'm not careful, I'm left feeling disappointed after each window-shopping trip, like my home would be oh-so-lovely if I could just buy all. the. things. Or even just a couple of them.

While we can blame TV networks, advertising campaigns, and the "impulse buy" section of stores for fueling our quest for more, it's also driven by social media. We may feel like we can trust the recommendations of influencers and our online "friends," but how many of those social media interactions leave us feeling discontented and wanting more things? How many times have we felt unhappy with our lives after we've scrolled our newsfeeds? For me, it's often easy to admire what someone else has and question why I can't or don't have the same.

Thanks to social media, covetousness abounds today. Consider the time we've spent checking out our friends' profiles only to find ourselves struggling with envy ("I want that!") or pride ("Mine is so much better than that!"). Before we realize it, we're filled with a strong desire for someone else's possessions, whether her kitchen or her vacation or her stunning outfit. We're eager to get what someone else has or to do what someone else does at all costs. That couch we envied in our high school friend's photo? If we could just pick up a side hustle (or two) and fit it into our (already-filled) schedule, maybe we could earn enough money to buy something just like it.

Whether intentionally created by high-paid advertising execs or unintentionally fostered by social media, all the propaganda leaves us feeling like we need what's different or better for our homes and our lives. Every single December and February I'm tricked into thinking my life could be better with extravagant diamond jewelry just because of the commercials I see on TV. Although I'm savvy enough to see through the obscene push for more in these ads, it's impossible to completely avoid experiencing the temptation. And the push for more never stops. Unless we ban ourselves from watching TV or unsubscribe from most email lists, the encouragement to buy more comes every single day.

Tension Tamer

Advertising and social media leave me feeling like my reality is flawed or that I must be doing something wrong. I'm tempted to believe that I always need to do more, be more, or have more. Do you feel it too?

To help you loosen the tight grip of commercialism on your own life and break free from the trap of feeling compelled to buy what you see, keep a watchful eye out for compelling ads and commercials. They're everywhere. Start noticing which ads create the biggest distractions or temptations for you. When you see those ads, observe how desperately retailers want you to spend money.

The trick to breaking free from the quest for more can be found in identifying lies and replacing them with the Lord's truth. King David wrote about this freedom in Psalm 40:4–5:

> Blessed is the man who makes
>   the LORD his trust,
> who does not turn to the proud,
>   to those who go astray after a lie!
> You have multiplied, O LORD my God,
>   your wondrous deeds and your thoughts toward us;
>   none can compare with you!
> I will proclaim and tell of them,
>   yet they are more than can be told.

The Lord multiplies his wondrous deeds and thoughts toward us. When we glorify our homes and possessions, we try to replace those wonderful blessings with shoddy substitutes. It's like we're trying to quickly satisfy our ravenous hunger with cheap drive-thru burgers and fries when scrumptious and satisfying farm-to-table feasts have already been freshly prepared for us.

As David revealed, when we make the *Lord* our trust, we'll stop going after the lie. We'll break free from the quest for more and begin to walk in contentment.

Cutting the Ties to Temptation

Of course, any sincere Christian would happily say she wants to make the Lord her trust, but what practical steps can help this become a reality? How can we take what we understand and start living it out?

One place to begin is by limiting our exposure to what influences our quest for more. If we need a more extreme approach, we can choose to completely avoid—either for a limited time or permanently—the culprits that encourage our compulsion to buy.

I'm a firm believer that radical changes can make huge differences when necessary. For instance, years ago I stopped all nonessential shopping trips for six months. At that time in my life, whenever I'd had an especially hard day (which, as a mom of toddlers, happened multiple times a week!), I'd stop by my favorite stores to wander the aisles, looking for distractions in the form of appealing objects. To try to cope with my stress, I'd end up buying something I didn't truly need, which only added to my family's credit card debt and collection of stuff. After looking at the climbing bills every month and recognizing that I didn't even truly like my spur-of-the-moment purchases, I knew I needed to stop. But I kept walking into the stores tired, stressed, and without the willpower to avoid making unnecessary purchases.

I decided to try a one-month personal challenge to skip the tempting aisles and only buy essential items. After one month I extended my challenge to three months, then to six. During my shopping fast, I either avoided the areas of the stores where I typically spent money on things I didn't need, or I stayed away from my usual haunts altogether.

Only when I forced myself to stop buying all nonessentials for a season did I realize I had had an addiction to retail therapy.

Aside from avoidance, how did I overcome this addiction? Well, a huge difference came from a changed heart. Once I embraced this shift in my shopping habits, I realized that I finally had enough after years of accumulating belongings. My home was already filled with things I enjoyed. Enough was enough. Buying one more item for an already-filled house would mean that I'd need to get rid of something I loved to make room for the new.

After years of battling my reliance on retail therapy, I can now walk through home departments and appreciate the beauty of the merchandise. And, miracle of miracles, unless I have something on my shopping list, I can walk through without making a purchase! I'm not completely immune to the marketing, though. Like with many things in life, most days I can avoid giving in to temptation, but in moments of weakness, I find myself caving in. But after years of giving in to the temptation to buy beautiful but unnecessary things, it's thrilling to finally possess the willpower to resist.

Granted, I still really appreciate using a new purchase, but I'm not a better person because I have a new coffee mug or pillow. My belongings don't make me feel fulfilled. Even if what I own makes me smile, these things don't complete me.

This experience has shown me that the cold-turkey approach is an incredibly effective way for me to begin to change my life. Similarly, during the height of the pandemic, I discovered that I wrestled with awful feelings about people on social media who I cared about in real life. One day, with my tried-and-true cold-turkey approach, I unfriended every single friend and stayed off for almost an entire year. While this might sound a bit dramatic, I can't begin to describe how incredibly freeing a life without social media felt! But I didn't stay away forever. Eventually my negative feelings cooled down. When I felt like I'd resolved my anxiety, anger, and comparison issues, I returned to social media, and now I have a much more positive experience. At the time, though, I knew it was creating a lot of temptation and sin in my life. To break free, I had to cut off everything.

In a way, this felt like living out Jesus's teaching from the Sermon on the Mount:

> If your right eye causes you to sin, tear it out and throw it away. For it is better that you lose one of your members than that your whole body be thrown into hell. And if your right

hand causes you to sin, cut it off and throw it away. For it is better that you lose one of your members than that your whole body go into hell. (Matt. 5:29–30)

Some days I felt that skipping my comforting shopping trips or quitting social media was as painful as tearing out and throwing away my eyeball! But I'm glad I did it.

Tension Tamer

If you're tempted by the quest for more every time you open your inbox, unsubscribe from promotional emails. Before you turn on the TV, consider what you're planning to watch. If you know you'll end up binge-watching a favorite show that typically fills you with envy or a desire for more, it would be wise to find something else to watch that won't cause you to fall into temptation. Or even to take a complete break from TV for a while. If social media fuels something not-so-great in your life, try unfollowing the people and brands who regularly ignite jealousy or anger or covetousness in you.

You may not need an extreme cold-turkey approach like I did. To figure what might work for you, take some time to consider your own home and experiences with shopping:

- What are some of your biggest stumbling blocks?
- Are you tempted by the simplicity of one-click purchases or the thrill of scouring the internet for irresistible finds? Or is

your temptation something altogether different?

- What are the retail and marketing temptations that trip you?
- What emotional triggers compel you to buy?
- How can you break free from any of these material addictions and, as David described in Psalm 40:4, not go astray after a lie?
- How can you begin to make the Lord your trust instead of relying on your retail habits?

I can't answer these questions for you, but I hope that asking yourself is helpful as you create your own approach.

Staying in Your Lane

Limiting—or eliminating—the sources of the temptation to rely on our belongings or homes is a great first step. But here's a second approach that will keep our eyes focused on the Lord's activity in our lives: reminding ourselves to stay in our own lanes.

Paul encouraged the Corinthian church to do this in his first letter to them:

Don't you realize that in a race everyone runs, but only one person gets the prize? So run to win! All athletes are disciplined in their training. They do it to win a prize that will fade away, but we do it for an eternal prize. So I run with purpose in every step. I am not just shadowboxing. I discipline my body like an athlete, training it to do what it should. Otherwise, I fear that after preaching to others I myself might be disqualified. (1 Corinthians 9:24–27 NLT)

What does this kind of discipline and self-control look like? Discipline means running our own races—the unique race the Lord has set out just for you or me. I encourage you to find comfort in the fact that the race of your life is unique. No one else has your exact gifts and abilities. You're the only one with your set of strengths and weaknesses. And you're the only one with your particular call on your life. If you spend your time and attention watching how other people live, you end up taking your eyes off your *own* race.

If we were competing in a race, glancing at our competitors would mean we're taking our focus off our own lanes and zeroing in on others', causing us to drift and lose valuable time. Similarly, if we're cruising down the highway, we need to stay in our own lanes. The cars of our dreams may come speeding up behind us, but we'll face consequences if we shift our attention to those other cars. Chances are we'd drift into another lane, and the results could be catastrophic.

No matter how fancy another person's house and belongings are, it's important that you and I remain focused on our own races. As we stay in our lanes and give our attention to what the Lord has brought into our specific lives and homes, we'll be happier and more content. We'll be able to use our seasons of life and our personal and material gifts for his glory. And we will begin to live a life free from the tension of the quest for more.

Tension Tamer

To help you find freedom from the tension of the quest for more, now's a fantastic time to contemplate what fuels dissatisfaction in you the most.

Identifying the culprit is the first step:

- When do you most often catch yourself wishing to have something else or be like someone else?
- Are specific people, brands, or platforms on social media sticking in your thoughts in an unhealthy way?

The next step is figuring out ways to deal with these temptations:

- What actions do you need to take today to find freedom?
- Do you need to go hardcore and quit cold turkey? Press the delete button? Unsubscribe from mailing lists?
- How can you keep reminding yourself to stay in your own lane?
- How can you run with purpose in every step?

Taking action might feel difficult, but try to begin today. It's the first step on the path to freedom.

Chapter 3

Peers

ICK. THE ALL-too-familiar feeling that started in middle school reared its ugly head again. The uncomfortable impression that I didn't belong was back with a vengeance. I felt like everyone else had been invited to hang out except me, only this time the exclusion wasn't at cafeteria tables with a bunch of awkward and mean preteen girls. This time it happened at church with a bunch of grown women. Weren't we supposed to be sisters in Christ?

Maybe my family couldn't break into the crowd because we'd just moved to the area and hadn't been part of their small groups since we were newlyweds like the rest of them had. Maybe we were excluded because our kids hadn't been born into that church. Maybe it was something altogether different. My head was tired of thinking through the reasons I would be kept at a distance in this body of Christ.

But all my wondering didn't change reality. In the one place where my family hoped to feel safe, welcomed, and accepted, we were treated like outsiders.

Finally, in what seemed like a miracle, a mom from church invited me to a purse party in her home. I scoured my closet to find a good moms'-night-out outfit, kissed my husband and babies goodbye, and left for my evening away. Maybe since the attendees were all moms who recognized the importance of raising our young children in the church, I could break into this circle of friends.

At the time, my family was pinching pennies on my husband's teacher salary, and I was grateful for our family's simple split-level home. I wasn't mentally prepared to show up to a starter castle. Was I dressed okay? Would I know what to talk about? I gathered my courage, knocked on the front door, and hoped my smile would disguise my fear. Once I sat down at the party, I tried to start conversations with other women. But everyone else already knew each other and picked right up in their friendships. Few women asked me questions or attempted to get to know me, so I did a lot of listening, smiling, and nodding.

When I eyeballed the price tags of the purses, I prayed I didn't look too shocked. I wanted to get up, walk straight out the front door, and drive home to my family as fast as I could, but I forced myself to sit there and pretend I was both having a good time and could afford any of the purses. Yet all the pretending in the world couldn't make me feel better about spending my family's carefully budgeted money on a purse I didn't even like. At the end of the party, I ordered the smallest change purse available, tried to navigate cordial goodbye conversations, and drove home feeling like an absolute phony.

That night I discovered it doesn't matter what age you are. Even though I was well into my thirties and thought I had moved past my middle school people-pleasing pangs, the same insecurity came surging back in the name of trying to fit in with a new crowd.

Checking Your Influences

You may wonder how the awkwardly painful subject of mom cliques has anything to do with the tension of caring for your home. But it's simple: Sometimes where we live or how we live has everything to do with the way people welcome us into their lives—or the way we hope to fit into theirs.

Is this ridiculous and awful? Absolutely. But it's also accurate.

Now, not all peer pressure is bad. For example, the influence of others may be beneficial if you find yourself in an unexpected but healthy mentoring or accountability relationship. In the split-level where my husband and I raised our toddlers, all our neighbors were retirees who had plenty of time to work on their lawns and gardens. This was fairly new territory for my husband and me, and it was pretty intimidating to be surrounded by gorgeous landscaping. One day my next-door neighbor mentioned she was ready to start working in "our" neighbor garden. Apparently, she and the previous owners of my home had created a garden on the boundary line between the two properties.

I'm pretty sure I never would've volunteered myself to take care of a neighbor garden; after all, I was a mom to two toddlers and didn't think I had time for gardening. But my new neighbor was kind enough to teach me all she knew. We'd talk and get to know each other as we spent hours digging, weeding, and appreciating our beautiful flower garden together, and I learned unforgettable gardening and life lessons because of all the time spent with my dear neighbor. The unexpected pressure I faced to maintain our neighbor garden ended up in a wonderful friendship.

However, when the pressure to fit in with your peers only wears you out and causes you to spend a bunch of money, an entirely new layer of tension is created. Navigating the world of women's relationships is hard enough, but when you start inviting others' expectations into your home, suddenly someone else is influencing your decisions, and they don't even live with you, chip in with housework, or help pay the bills.

You may not think you wrestle with giving in to peer pressure, but have you ever:

- Felt convinced you needed to move to a certain neighborhood or a specific street to be able to better fit in with someone?
- Wanted to buy something for your home, whether a fern or a welcome sign or an extensive bathroom remodel, only because your friends have it?
- Questioned if you could plan the "right" menu or have a nice enough or clean enough or updated enough house to invite people over for dinner?
- Thought you needed to keep up the appearance of your house to the standards of your friend group (or the group you are trying to get accepted into) by hiring a lawn service, cleaning lady, or some other professional?

Let's be clear: If you can't do specific home tasks and truly need a professional to help, hire the help! If you've always dreamed of a particular furnishing that others also happen to have and you have the money for it, make the purchase. If your family is ready to pack up and move and you find a house in your budget that also happens to be in a popular location, do what's best for your family. If you can make those choices with contentment and the Lord is glorified, go for it! But if you're feeling *pressured* into a choice just because "everyone else is doing it" or you want it to boost your popularity, now's the perfect time to evaluate and adjust your priorities.

Even as a woman who tends to go against the flow, I've had to make plenty of hard home decisions based solely on financial criteria. As much as I felt tempted to try to fit in and move to a certain part of town or get a specific home renovation to better relate to my friends, I've had to slam the brakes on keeping up with the Joneses. Fortunately, my husband isn't swayed by emotional choices. Although it's been difficult at times to disagree and follow his lead, it's worked out for the best— even if and when I pout about needing to make an unpopular choice that none of my peers needs to make.

Tension Tamer

Tensions from pleasing people are real. But they're not impossible to overcome. With some introspection, you may be able to uncover who adds pressure to your life and how you can move past this pattern.

- **Do you find yourself trying to keep up with any of your friends or acquaintances? In what ways?**
- **If you feel pressure to keep up with others, what could you do this week to try to stay in your own lane?**

Using Transparency to Your Advantage

In today's culture of online influences, you might think the pressure to fit in is something new brought on by social media. But it's not. The Bible is filled with accounts of people being influenced by others, both positively and negatively. Think of the way Esau was impacted by Jacob, Samson was influenced by Delilah, and the Israelites were persuaded by ten of the twelve men Moses sent out to explore Canaan.[1]

Sometimes the true source of the pressure we feel to fit in has less to do with our friends and their possessions and actually much more to do with our maturity in Christ and our own sinful human nature. Remember the Ten Commandments? Exodus 20:17 directly tells us, "You shall not covet your neighbor's house." The matter doesn't get any clearer than that! As much as we might wish biblical words on this matter would include our getting whatever we desire, that's simply not the case.

While the tensions of peer pressure, comparison, and insecurity can seem pretty powerful, there is a way to break free. It takes courage and determination, though. We can begin to avoid comparisons by choosing to live with transparency.

We all face unique circumstances, but everyone struggles and is imperfect. When we're going through a rough patch, we don't have to put up a phony front and make things seem better than they are. It's okay to admit our struggles and imperfections. Transparency about these challenges is a good thing, and it's desperately needed in this world.

On the flip side, we don't have to accentuate the negative in our lives or make things seem worse than they are. When all is going well, let's celebrate! It's okay to be grateful for the good in our lives, and it's not boasting when we appreciate what we like about our homes.

One easy and enjoyable way to live with transparency is by hosting friends. I'm not necessarily talking about women we've just met, but our true friends. Instead of cleaning our houses for hours ahead of time, let's try *not* cleaning. Invite others into our messes. If we ask someone over at the last minute and our counters are cluttered or our sinks are splattered, it's okay. Real life happens to everyone. We don't have to pretend we have everything in our lives together. Let's not skimp on investing in relationships simply because we feel like our homes aren't "perfect" enough to let people into. Open the door and don't be afraid to be your true self.

Looking at Others with Love

Unfortunately, much like I discovered that feelings of insecurity pop up at all ages and stages of life, judgment isn't isolated to adolescence. I'm the first to admit I've struggled as an adult with feelings of judgment and preference toward the women around me, even when these thoughts make absolutely no sense. When I think or act like this, I'm completely ignoring what James warned against in his letter to the early church:

My dear brothers and sisters, how can you claim to have faith in our glorious Lord Jesus Christ if you favor some people over others?

For example, suppose someone comes into your meeting dressed in fancy clothes and expensive jewelry, and another comes in who is poor and dressed in dirty clothes. If you give special attention and a good seat to the rich person, but you say to the poor one, "You can stand over there, or else sit on the floor"—well, doesn't this discrimination show that your judgments are guided by evil motives? (James 2:1-4 NLT)

Our choices may not be based on a simple rich-versus-poor division like James wrote about, but we all have women we'd rather not be around and others we want to be our best friends.

Fortunately for you and me, the Lord is gracious and can teach us— even if the lessons seem to come ever so slowly—how to see others with grace and love no matter how different they seem. As we learn from Jesus's gentle instruction, we'll live out the commandment he gave his disciples in John 13:34-35: "A new command I give you: Love one another. As I have loved you, so you must love one another. By this everyone will know that you are my disciples, if you love one another" (NIV). Let's let people know that we're Christ's disciples by loving them well.

Tension Tamer

Do you see judgmental attitudes cropping up in your own thoughts, words, and behaviors? How have you felt when you faced the judgment of another woman?

Looking in the Mirror

What if our preconceived ideas and opposition have nothing to do with what's wrong with someone else and absolutely everything to do with what's wrong with us? Ugly feelings of jealousy, envy, and covetousness can sour even what started out as a friendship. How is this possible? We might covet, or inordinately desire, our neighbor's house. We could envy, or resentfully desire, our friend's marriage or career.

When we see a friend obtain something we didn't even know we wanted—whether it's a strong marriage, a tropical vacation, new furniture, a job promotion, or home improvements—it's easy to start accentuating that friend's personal weaknesses as a way to diminish the perceived happiness in her life. If we imagine enough bad things about her, maybe we'll feel better about ourselves, right?

When we realize these obsessions and wishes are sinful, we might stop ourselves in our tracks. However, if we keep harboring feelings of jealousy about our friend because her house or marriage or career appeals to us, those feelings might morph into hostility. All that jealousy creates a real problem as we end up searching for personal faults in our friend just because we started off admiring something she owned.

David addressed what we should do about all this in Psalm 15:1–5 (NLT) when he wrote,

Who may worship in your sanctuary, LORD?
    Who may enter your presence on your holy hill?
Those who lead blameless lives and do what is right,
    speaking the truth from sincere hearts.
Those who refuse to gossip
    or harm their neighbors
    or speak evil of their friends.
Those who despise flagrant sinners,
    and honor the faithful followers of the LORD,
    and keep their promises even when it hurts.
Those who lend money without charging interest,
    and who cannot be bribed to lie about the innocent.
Such people will stand firm forever.

If we slow down to unpack the truth found in this psalm, we discover that those who choose to live blameless and right lives may worship the Lord in his sanctuary. But how can we live blamelessly? What are some of those right patterns of life the Lord approves of?

As David explained, refusing to gossip is essential, along with refusing to speak evil of our friends. Even if we're in the middle of a huge internal battle against envying our neighbor's latest purchase, we should *not* talk to others about the purchase. Even if we wonder how in the world our friend can afford to remodel her home, we should *not* gossip about the renovations.

Thinking and speaking the truth is vital. Even if we wish we had a different life or a nicer home, we shouldn't spin our friend's good fortune and personal decisions into something negative just to make ourselves feel better.

It's important to keep our promises, even if and when it hurts. Don't lie about the innocent. Lend money without charging interest. Honor the Lord's faithful followers. And without speaking evil, despise flagrant sinners.

Now is the time to stop the assumptions and judgment. What if we ended the mental comparison games and could just celebrate with our friends? If we're brutally honest, all of this can be a tough order. Let's look again to the Psalms to discover how we can go to the Lord to help us accomplish this.

Stopping the Mean Girl Within

As a man who experienced friendships gone wrong, King David knew the agony of betrayal. He knew how much it hurt. And he poured out his heart to the Lord in Psalm 109:1–5 (NIV):

> My God, whom I praise,
>   do not remain silent,
> for people who are wicked and deceitful

> have opened their mouths against me;
>   they have spoken against me with lying tongues.
> With words of hatred they surround me;
>   they attack me without cause.
> In return for my friendship they accuse me,
>   but I am a man of prayer.
> They repay me evil for good,
>   and hatred for my friendship.

Women can be strange. They're sometimes catty. Or particular. You don't always know where you stand or what you did to get on their bad side or good side. Whether they're Christian or not, women may be for you—or they may be against you. But instead of continually competing in some sort of brutal contest where everyone makes up their own rules that they don't share with anyone else, what if we started rooting for each other?

One practical and simple solution to overcoming these competitive thoughts is making a conscious choice to be the change. Sincerely encourage others. Get used to saying the phrase, "I'm cheering you on," and meaning what you say. If you admire something in your friend's home, tell her. Instead of morphing into some sort of creepy green-eyed monster, try to genuinely appreciate what your friend has.

Tension Tamer

Who do you need to start encouraging? What's one specific way you can cheer on that person this week?

Another game-changing realization we can have is that every single woman on this planet deals with challenges and weaknesses. As Melanie Dale explains in her book *Women Are Scary*:

When we see each other out of context of our home lives, we can assume that everyone else has it all together and we're the only ones hanging on by a thread. The truth is, so many of us are messy and cracked. We're just afraid to talk about it.

We all judge other women and are judged in return. Other moms judge our kids, our parenting choices, our appearance. Even when we don't mean to, we make snap decisions about other women, and we're so dang intimidating to one another.[2]

In light of this, how can we start showing each other more compassion? Instead of imagining what compels other women to behave in certain ways, let's give more grace. Rather than assuming a woman has a perfect life based on outer appearances, let's keep in mind that we have no idea what she's really facing. And instead of supposing that a woman who looks like she's not holding everything together is a hot mess, let's remember that every single one of us is far from perfect.

Learn from David's painful experience: Don't be a bad friend. Don't be a mean girl. Don't lie and attack others or spread accusations as a two-faced frenemy. If you feel tempted to repay your friend's goodness with evil, stop. Choose to glorify the Lord in your friendships by treating others with respect and kindness, even when you feel a twinge (or a crashing wave) of jealousy.

As we choose to become good friends and kind, loving ambassadors of Christ to this world, we'll start the process of breaking free from the tension from our peers.

Chapter 4

Family

Growing up, I loved spending time at my grandparents' house. Set in a quaint small town, their house was large and packed with old-fashioned charm. While a big part of the welcoming atmosphere definitely was established by my kind and loving grandma, I also loved the spacious rooms, hardwood floors, and built-ins. From the time I was a little girl, I imagined buying the house someday and making it my own.

When I actually grew up and it was time for my widowed grandma to move from her house, my husband, Aaron, and I were interested in buying it. Sure, it needed updated heating and cooling and windows, but it would be an amazing place to live for decades to come. My grandma even planned to sell it for a great price. Yet, as much as I hoped something could work out, it was out of our price range.

I cried the last time I walked through the house, remembering all the wonderful family memories in each room and realizing that I'd never be back inside. But once my grandma completely moved out and the house was sold to the new owners, Aaron shared how relieved he was. While it definitely would've been an incredible house for us, he admitted he would've felt pressured to host all the family gatherings.

And while we would've wanted to make the house our own, he feared who might be offended if we changed the wall colors or made any cosmetic updates.

People move into homes all the time that have been passed down from family members, so changing things is not an impossibility. But Aaron also brought up an incredibly valid point about the tension we all face in our homemaking that stems from family influences and expectations.

Tension Tamer

What aspects of your homemaking are based on the expectation of relatives who don't even live with you?

While the pressure from our friends and their belongings can add tension to the way we view our homes, family members can create a unique kind of people-pleasing pressure. I'm talking about influences from parents, siblings, and extended family members—I'll talk about the tension from kids and spouses in later chapters. While pressures from friends can be intense, the tension created by your family can be epic.

Each of us knows, more than anyone else, our own family's dynamics. We know the hot-button issues that get them going and the conflicting personalities that cause people to walk on eggshells around each other. We've experienced their comfort as well as their criticism. And we're keenly aware of certain family members who are standoffish about our homes, others who are completely up in our business and persistently give suggestions, or others who simply encourage and praise our hard work. We may even be able to recall their exact words about our homes, whether compliments or critiques.

Because family ties can be so close, our relatives may feel the liberty to chime in with their opinions. Without being asked they may not shy away from explaining exactly how we need to do something in our homes, from loading the dishwasher the "right" way, to which color we should paint a room, to "properly" scrubbing the floor. If we're struggling to figure things out on our own, their guidance can be priceless. But other times, we might not want the instruction. For instance, matters can grow very complicated if we get unsolicited advice on the exact way to negotiate a housing offer.

Going Your Own Way

Some of my dear friends and mentors at church were talking with me about the importance and delicate balance of supporting and encouraging adult children while stepping back as moms. Then they shared horror stories of their own life experiences. One eighty-year-old friend told about the astonishment she had when she brought her firstborn child home from the hospital. While she had been in the hospital with her baby, her husband and mother-in-law had moved the family's belongings from one apartment to another without ever consulting her! Understandably, coming "home" from the hospital to an entirely new location infuriated that new mom.

Another friend, busy juggling life as a wife and mom, was shocked to come home one day and find her kitchen cupboards completely rearranged without her knowledge or approval. Her mother-in-law had come over while the family was out for the day and had cleaned and rearranged the kitchen without ever being asked. She simply thought to herself that it needed to be done.

The takeaway from my conversations that day was clear: Our family members might think they're helping us by working in our homes, but even though they have good intentions, they end up overstepping boundaries and encroaching on our independence.

Tension Tamer

If you're a parent of grown children, it's so important to step back and maintain boundaries. Verbally give them freedom to do their own thing, then truly let them make their choices and manage their homes. Love and encourage them. Pray for them. Be a part of their lives. But be careful not to overstep reasonable boundaries.

If you're a parent of young children, make a commitment now that when the time comes and your kids are grown and gone, you'll let them make their own decisions and maintain their own homes.

Maybe your family members haven't meddled overtly in your housekeeping, but you might feel pressured to do things their way in other aspects. It's okay to make your own decisions. You can choose to respectfully listen to their advice, but you don't have to take it. Being a child or grandchild does *not* mean you need to live a lifetime of childlike obedience to your elders.

Though it can be challenging, it is possible to go your own way. We can create unique lives, relationships, and homes that still honor and respect our family members. Be sure to pray for the Lord's leading and guidance. What would bring him the most glory? What truly matters? Take time to consider what you'd prefer to do. Examine your motives, pray about the situation, and then make your choice.

When you make a decision that isn't in line with what your family has suggested, it's appropriate to prepare yourself for their hurt feelings, disappointment, or disagreement. But remember that you don't need to please people with obedience. Gently but firmly resist the pressure to give in while respectfully honoring your family members. Just as they made choices for their lives, you have the opportunity to as well.

Asserting your independence may feel like an awkward or difficult transition, especially if you've typically done what your family members have advised. If a family member tends to be bossy, standing up to any sort of resistance from them might feel like a huge clash of personalities. But here's the thing: Our homes are *our* homes. If we're living financially independent from our extended families, we get to make decisions and create and maintain the home we want, any way we want to do it. (Financial dependence comes with its own unique set of issues.)

If relationships become strained over your decision, know you're not alone. David wrote in Psalm 27:7–10 (NIV):

> Hear my voice when I call, LORD;
>   be merciful to me and answer me.
> My heart says of you, "Seek his face!"
>   Your face, LORD, I will seek.
> Do not hide your face from me,
>   do not turn your servant away in anger;
>   you have been my helper.
> Do not reject me or forsake me,
>   God my Savior.
> Though my father and mother forsake me,
>   the LORD will receive me.

Lord willing, your father and mother will not forsake you, especially over trivial matters like what you serve for Mother's Day brunch or how you furnish your home. If they already have and they're still living, you certainly can pray for restoration. As Psalm 34:14 counsels, "Seek peace and pursue it." If they've forsaken you and have since passed away, you can forgive them and pray for the Lord to mend your emotional wounds.

Examining Your Defaults

Even if you come from a family that encourages independence, there's still a good probability you've been conditioned to care for your home a certain way. Like it or not, we've all been influenced in how we care for and think about our homes based on the way we were raised.

We can become more aware of our unconscious defaults if we consider an old fable that tells the story of a newlywed couple:

One night at dinner, a husband asked his new bride why she cut off the ends of their pot roast before cooking it. She answered that it's simply the way to make pot roast—this was the way her mother always did it.

When the young wife asked her mother why *she* cut off the ends of the pot roast, her mother answered that *her* mother always did it that way. So the young wife decided to ask her grandmother the secret behind cutting off the ends of pot roasts, and her grandmother answered that *her* mother always did this.

Curious to find the reason behind her great-grandmother's cooking secrets, the bride visited the elderly woman and asked about the family's pot roast tradition. Her great-grandmother's answer? "I cut off the ends of my pot roast so it would fit into the small baking dish I had."

So often we're just like the young bride, dutifully following the homemaking methods of our mothers or grandmothers—or even great-grandmothers!—just because they were modeled to us in that way. Maybe some of their tried-and-true methods *are* the best. But do we know this for sure? Could a different way be better? Would another way suit our homes or our preferences better?

After assuming for years that I needed to use all the cleaning products and techniques that I learned from my mom, I started trying new things. For about ten years of my adult housekeeping life, I used dusting spray like my mom had taught me when I was a kid. She never told me I needed to continue dusting this way; I just assumed it was the only way. After a while, I realized there might be alternatives to this technique. I finally ditched the aerosol sprays I used for my childhood chores, switched to a microfiber dusting mitt, and have never looked back.

Old habits can be hard to break, especially when we aren't even aware they're habits. It might take us years—or decades—to realize that there's a different way that directly contradicts a belief or practice we've never before questioned. As embarrassing as it sounds, it's literally taken me more than thirty years to realize that specific ways of maintaining a house that were modeled by my parents aren't the only right way to do things. And even if I find a certain way I enjoy tending to my home, I need to remember it's not the only way. Someday I might find a better solution. If and when I do, I hope I'm quick to change my habits.

Do you feel like you need to cook or clean or decorate exactly like other family members always have? Maybe it's time to try something else to see if it works better for you!

If you feel like you need permission to establish new routines and habits and ways of doing things in your home, consider this your green light. Your grandma might have been the queen of clean, and you could learn a thing or two from her example, but now could also be the perfect time to figure things out for yourself. Your mom might be the most amazing cook you know, but you can improvise on her recipes. Your sister might love a certain decorative aesthetic or organizational approach, but what works for her might be the opposite of what you choose in your home.

Truly, there's no dishonor in doing things your own way. It's okay.

Breaking your family's mold and living with your own choices can seem a little scary. After all, will your decision hurt someone else's feelings? Aren't you expected to go along with traditions?

Here's the freeing truth: You can embrace your family's traditions as much or as little as you'd like while you create the home you want and need.

If you're married, you could even ask your mother-in-law how she managed her home and then try some of her secrets. You never know what might work out for you! Without feeling pressured by others, select what's best for you, your family, and your home.

Tension Tamer

What is one cleaning method you use because you were trained to do it that way as a child? What is one way you prepare food because of the specific way that a family member taught you?

Starting from Scratch

For as much as families can influence us and our approaches to our homes, some of us might not have experienced much positive family input as we were growing up. Maybe you never learned what was needed to care for a home or how to tend to everyday tasks. Perhaps the only lesson you ever learned from your parents was what *not* to do in life. Maybe you're alone today either by choice or circumstance. If you don't have the influence or pressure of family members, one of your biggest difficulties may involve wishing someone would speak into your home decisions. You might wish you had some kind of a role model to act as a guide.

While you long for a different reality, there is biblical comfort. As the psalmist wrote in Psalm 146:5–9,

> Blessed is he whose help is the God of Jacob,
>   whose hope is in the LORD his God,

who made heaven and earth,
    the sea, and all that is in them,
who keeps faith forever;
    who executes justice for the oppressed,
who gives food to the hungry.

The LORD sets the prisoners free;
    the LORD opens the eyes of the blind.
The LORD lifts up those who are bowed
        down;
    the LORD loves the righteous.
The LORD watches over the sojourners;
    he upholds the widow and the fatherless.

When you hope in the Lord, he can be your help. He remains faithful and provides what you need, whether it's justice or food, freedom or sight. God will watch over you and uphold you. He loves you.

I fully believe he will provide the wisdom and insight you need. It might be a creative way, like information you seek out from a credible source. He might bring a mentor into your life who can help advise you and weigh difficult decisions. Or he may answer your prayers in a completely surprising way when you least expect it. Ask the Lord for wisdom. Ask him for guidance and help. Then pay attention and see the ways he will provide.

Tension Tamer

What basic homemaking or housekeeping skills do you want to learn? Who could you ask for help? What resources could you investigate to learn how to do what you want to know?

Leaving and Cleaving

When I consider familial cleaning habits, I remember all too well what it felt like to be a newlywed getting settled into my new home and thinking, "But my parents never did things this way!" The changes that come with being a newlywed remind me of the truth in another psalm written by the Sons of Korah:

> Listen, daughter, and pay careful attention:
>   Forget your people and your father's house.
> Let the king be enthralled by your beauty;
>   honor him, for he is your lord.
>   (Psalm 45:10–11 NIV)

British pastor Charles Spurgeon explains that Psalm 45 is "no wedding song of earthly nuptials" but rather describes "the heavenly Bridegroom and His elect spouse."[1] We can learn so many spiritual lessons from these few verses. One such lesson is that we need to actively listen and pay careful attention to the Lord. It's vital to obey and honor his righteous commands. And when we follow Christ, we need to leave behind our former ways of life.

Yet Psalm 45 also includes incredibly practical, everyday advice for any wife. Once married, a husband and wife become their *own* family. Your marriage has the potential to glorify God, and it doesn't need to reflect the wishes or traditions of your parents or your in-laws. You can forget the ways of your people and your father's house.

As the Lord commanded in Genesis 2:24, "For this reason a man shall leave his father and his mother, and be joined to his wife; and they shall become one flesh" (NASB). This call to leave our parents and cleave to our spouses is crucial in marriage. And it's crucial in our homes. When we're leaving and cleaving, we can start fresh and create our own family and household. Doing this is more than okay—it's biblical.

If you feel pressured into choosing the home of your parents' dreams for you, rethink that decision. Instead of feeling like you're obligated to carry on your parents' or grandparents' holiday traditions, let that tension go. Create your own family traditions if you'd like. Are you bending under the weight or sheer magnitude of all your family's heirlooms and antique furniture? Remember that every possession was new at some point. Just like one of your ancestors chose to acquire that belonging, you can choose to pass the treasure along so someone else can appreciate it.

When I was fresh out of college, I loved inheriting furniture from my grandparents and great-grandparents because it was a free way to furnish my apartments with durable furniture. My grandparents appreciated getting the old furniture out of their homes too. I didn't take everything I was offered, but over the years, I ended up keeping many of the pieces, yet not out of guilt or family pressure. Rather, I love the quality of the solid wood furniture. And instead of looking like a mismatched hodgepodge of freebies in my home, the pieces blend in with the rest of my style.

If you're not a fan of the furniture or belongings your family tries to pass along, don't feel pressured to say yes to taking them into your home. Honoring your family doesn't have to include honoring their possessions. If you feel like you're trapped by your family's wishes or belongings, I urge you to break free from that tension. Now's the time to nurture relationships and memories without feeling the unnecessary burden of pleasing others by carrying on traditions or holding on to their stuff.

This freedom to choose what we keep reminds me a lot of oyster stew and banana cream pie, of all things. For decades, my mom's side of the family served oyster stew at Thanksgiving, and throughout my childhood oyster stew as a Thanksgiving appetizer seemed as traditional as turkey and stuffing. For my husband's family, tradition came in the form of a favorite Thanksgiving dessert. While other families typically sat down for pumpkin pie after a big turkey dinner, they'd enjoy a nice slice of banana cream pie.

After my husband and I got married, had children, and started hosting Thanksgiving dinners, we had the liberty to create our own menu. We could ask guests to bring specific dishes or opt to make whatever we wanted. Somewhere along the way, we dropped the oyster stew. But banana cream pie has become part of our tradition, along with pecan pie and my mom's recipe for cherry-cranberry pie. Someday our son and daughter will choose some of our holiday traditions to pass along to their families, while leaving others behind. They'll make their own choices, just as it should be.

Tension Tamer

What is one family tradition you always look forward to repeating? What is one family tradition you'd rather not pass along?

As freeing or frightening as the permission to change might feel, figuring out your own preferences is important because there's not one "right" way to care for a home. Choose what's best for your life. You don't have to try so hard to run your home just like the one you grew up in. Give yourself permission to attempt new methods and learn from both your successes and failures.

Ultimately, we don't need to seek approval from our family members. We need to seek it from the Lord. As Paul wrote in Galatians 1:10, "Am I now trying to win the approval of human beings, or of God? Or am I trying to please people? If I were still trying to please people, I would not be a servant of Christ" (NIV). When we break away from the tensions of people-pleasing, release ourselves from the expectations of others, stop trying to be just like someone else, and choose to seek the Lord, we'll experience joy and freedom beyond our wildest dreams as we create our *own* homes.

Chapter 5

Young Children

WHILE I WASN'T experiencing déjà vu, I certainly felt like I'd been through this identical scenario before. In fact, life seemed a little bit like *Groundhog Day*, where I experienced the same thing day after day after day. Regardless of how much I'd pick up before I went to bed at night, my home would look wrecked about twenty-two minutes after my toddler son and daughter woke up each morning. It didn't matter if I kept a little basket of toys in each room, all the toys in one playroom, or toys in their separate bedrooms—the mess multiplied and spread every single day.

I tried chore charts and reward systems. I tried purging toys. I tried teaching my kids how to pick up after themselves. I tried a rotation system that kept most of their toys in storage. I even tried ignoring the issue. But no matter what I tried, the result was the same—mess. And without fail, the mess led to massive feelings of frustration and overwhelm for me.

On the rare occasions when I tried slowing down to do some soul searching, I could easily dig to the root of my exasperation: unrealistic expectations.

Embracing Reality

So often as a mom I've dealt with frustration because the reality of raising my kids is nothing like I expected. At some point in my life, I bought into the myth that motherhood would be easy, and I'd instantly be a professional mom. Just like the familiar sentiment goes, I was an amazing expert in parenting before I had kids of my own. I was confident that once I became a mom, I would know the best way to discipline that was both effective and encouraging. Meals would be nutritious and delicious every day. Because they would love reading so much, my kids would never ask for screen time. And they'd want to help me clean the house.

Along with the wild idea that I'd somehow be a superior mom who knew just what to do and when to do it, I also imagined my kids would have different personalities and traits than they actually turned out to have. For example, I always thought that if I had a daughter, my little girl would want me to pick out her clothing (frilly dresses, of course) and braid her hair. What I didn't know was that when my daughter turned a year and a half old, she would know exactly what she wanted to wear every day, she most certainly didn't want me touching her hair, and she wasn't shy about communicating any of this. This ongoing struggle between our wills lasted for years until I was so tired of the trivial battles that I stepped back and stopped pestering her about outfits and hairdos. Now that she's a teen and has an amazing sense of style, I admire her determination and willingness to stand up for what she believes in. The traits that will serve her well as a woman have always been part of her feisty spirit, but back when I expected I'd have an easygoing, cooperative daughter, I was in for a surprise.

Whenever motherhood gets hard or my son or daughter veers off my fanciful, completely fictional course, I'm forced to acknowledge and embrace reality. Instead of pouting that my kids aren't how I imagined they might be, I need to welcome the fact that they're exactly the people God created them to be. Since God's plan is infinitely better than mine, it's a lot easier on my kids and me if I trust our Creator instead of forcing my own narrow hopes or dreams onto them. When I mentally create an idealized life where my kids always do what's best, our home is spotless, and I'm a perpetually cheerful mom who's always up for fun and games, it's like building a box and trying to neatly fit God, my kids, and myself into it. But what I actually need is for the Lord to rip that box to pieces and do *his* very good work in *his* very good way.

Once I started debunking my impractical parenting expectations, I could easily see how the ideals rubbed off on my perceptions of the way my home "should" be. Whether I wanted to accept it or not, the messiness that comes with children is a normal part of life. It doesn't mean I'm less of a mother, I have problem children, or my home looks like a disaster just because everyday life isn't neat and tidy. In fact, real, everyday life with kids is *not* neat and tidy for anyone.

Letting Kids Be Kids

When my kids were younger, my greatest consolation about my children's mess-making tactics was knowing I wasn't alone. Every other mom who had toddlers the same ages as mine dealt with the same issue, which eventually led me to a simple and relieving realization: Children are messy!

Though the messes in my home were frustrating, as I searched for ideas to help my kids clean up, I also found fascinating research proving that kids with messy rooms are more creative.[1] Plus, messy children learn more quickly.[2] As an adult, I prioritized a clean home because the order helped my own focus and peace. But my personal drive for cleanliness wasn't necessarily the best for my young kiddos.

Thinking back to my own childhood, I remembered what great fun I had playing to my heart's content with my toys. I'd fill my bedroom floor with what looked to anyone else like a huge mess. But I'd placed everything exactly where I wanted, in imaginary homes and towns all laid out in my mind.

With the help of these happy memories and the backing of scientific research, I found myself relaxing my neat-freak tendencies and extending much more grace in my home. My kids were able to learn by making messes, without having to endure constant nagging from their mom.

In my life, not much appeared to be different from the outside, but a massive change had happened in my *outlook*. While it was true that my husband and I still focused better, felt more cheerful, and experienced less stress in a clean environment, we also found freedom when we came to terms with the reality that making messes could actually benefit our kids.

This attitude of grace might be exactly what our children need. Instead of clutching on to the ideal of a perfect home or continually hovering over our young children to pick up what's out of place, relaxing our adult standards and letting kids be kids can free not only our children but also *ourselves*.

In the middle of mustering up grace to endure the mess, though, it can be helpful to remind yourself that this is a season. Your children won't always be this age. Their life stages will change, and they'll have other abilities and preferences. One day, they'll not only learn how to clean, but they also may even prefer a clean room. Even when messy days feel long, monotonous, and repetitive, a time will come when your kids will either willingly pick up or choose to get rid of the toys they've outgrown. Their tastes will change, and you'll help them transition from the innocent, creative fun of childhood to their maturing preferences.

When my own kids grew old enough to sell their unwanted toys at garage sales, outwardly I encouraged their decisions to downsize so they wouldn't hold on to possessions only to spare my feelings. Inwardly, though, I was sad to know that the moments of walking into my daughter's room and watching her play with teensy toy animals and dolls were over. My son was finished playing with his superhero toys. As long as the days might feel with young children, you won't have to tolerate your kids' messes forever.

Equipping Our Kids with Life Skills

In the middle of the messy preschool years, even when I realized a mess could be beneficial, I didn't completely give up on cleaning and live with a disaster of a home. I kept a nightly cleanup routine for myself so I could reset our home before the next day, and I still consistently tried to teach my son and daughter how to clean. Most days I needed to reteach them how to do basic chores and remind them to try to keep tidy.

Even with our parental frustrations and frazzled nerves, we need to remember that our children are young humans. They were created in the image of God, just like us. We don't need to talk down to them or insult them for what they haven't learned or mastered yet. Instead of begrudging them, we can speak blessing into their lives and then equip them with life skills and time for plenty of practice. Just like we weren't born with the knowledge of how to clean up after ourselves, neither were our kiddos. They need to be taught basic homemaking techniques too. In fact, I didn't learn some aspects of caring for my home until I was living on my own in my twenties. When I teach these skills to my kids, I try to share stories of times when I made some big mistakes learning how to do housework. Not only do these real-life examples add a whole lot of humor to the lessons, but they also help better pass along knowledge gained by years of experience.

If your kids truly are slobs and purposefully sabotage your cleaning efforts, you'll need to figure out motivations and methods to help them begin to learn. I wish I had a handy-dandy solution that works for every family, but I don't. Just like adults have different tolerances for clean and dirty, so do kids. Similarly, both kids and adults have a variety of motivations for cleaning up. It's a matter of trial and error to see what works best for your unique family. And keep in mind that what works well for you this week suddenly won't the next. As kids mature and change, their motivations and habits change as well.

This idea of growing maturity reminds me of the picture of families given in Psalm 127:3–5. After talking about the vanity of laboring without the Lord, here's how the psalmist described young families:

> Behold, children are a heritage from the LORD,
>   the fruit of the womb a reward.
> Like arrows in the hand of a warrior
>   are the children of one's youth.
> Blessed is the man
>   who fills his quiver with them!
> He shall not be put to shame
>   when he speaks with his enemies in the gate.

In other words, we're reminded to look at children as a share, inheritance, and gift from the Lord. They are his reward.

All that *fruit of the womb* and *children of one's youth* language? It reminds parents that this stage of life is a reward and blessing, because moms in the trenches need to remember this. When you're sleep-deprived and dealing with behavior issues and juggling the sheer mess of a quiverful of children, focusing on the challenges is easy. It's tempting to wish your current season of life away and dream you could transition to a different stage.

For years, I hated being a single young professional. Even though I was able to keep my apartment meticulously clean, my rooms seemed too quiet and empty. But when my prayers eventually were answered and I became a wife and then a mom, I missed having time just to myself, along with a quiet, clean, and calm living space. Everyone in my family had their preferences and needs, and they were not the same as my own! Yet the people and love and mess and noise that came with having my own family were exactly what I'd prayed for and longed for all those years.

There's no easy way around the fact that every single stage of life has unique challenges and disappointments. But at the same time, each season also has its own distinct joys and pleasures. In parenting, there are truly great aspects to nurturing a newborn, tending to a toddler, answering the countless questions of a little boy or girl, shepherding a school-aged child, and helping your growing teen transition into adulthood. The challenges in each phase can feel crushing, and circumstances can feel overwhelming—especially if we're juggling multiple children in various phases all at the same time. But let's keep reminding and encouraging ourselves: These challenges won't last forever.

Finding Strength for the Journey

When my son and daughter were young, the old Commodores' classic, "Easy (Like Sunday Morning)," made me laugh because there was absolutely nothing easy about a Sunday morning for me. My children would wake up at the crack of dawn six days a week, but without fail they slept in every Sunday. Once my husband and I would wake our kids up, the rush to feed them breakfast, get them dressed, have potty breaks, and get out the door in time for Sunday school seemed nearly impossible.

I remember trying to get a particularly moody and stubborn two-year-old out the door for church while she ran across our front sidewalk, screaming at the top of her lungs and trying to undress to her diaper. (*That* was quite a scene for our observant neighbors!) I remember screamy car rides. I remember silent, sulky car rides. I remember feeling so utterly exhausted that when we finally dropped our kids off at the church nursery and rushed into the sanctuary, I wanted to collapse into a pew.

Oddly enough, these Sunday morning memories help me relate

to the psalms known as the Songs of Ascents. Scholars believe these psalms, Psalms 120–134, were sung three times a year as the Israelites journeyed to Jerusalem for holy festivals: the Feast of the Passover in spring, the Feast of Pentecost in summer, and the Feast of Tabernacles in fall. The Israelites would've been familiar with the strain and struggle of getting all the family gathered and on the road in time to worship.

During their festival journeys, Israelites often traveled together in groups. We have a good record of one of these journeys since this kind of expedition was what Mary, Joseph, and Jesus were part of when they returned home from Jerusalem after the Feast of the Passover, as detailed in Luke 2:41–51:

> Every year Jesus' parents went to Jerusalem for the Passover festival. When Jesus was twelve years old, they attended the festival as usual. After the celebration was over, they started home to Nazareth, but Jesus stayed behind in Jerusalem. His parents didn't miss him at first, because they assumed he was among the other travelers. But when he didn't show up that evening, they started looking for him among their relatives and friends.
>
> When they couldn't find him, they went back to Jerusalem to search for him there. Three days later they finally discovered him in the Temple, sitting among the religious teachers, listening to them and asking questions. All who heard him were amazed at his understanding and his answers.
>
> His parents didn't know what to think. "Son," his mother said to him, "why have you done this to us? Your father and I have been frantic, searching for you everywhere."
>
> "But why did you need to search?" he asked. "Didn't you know that I must be in my Father's house?" But they didn't understand what he meant.

Then he returned to Nazareth with them and was obedient
to them. And his mother stored all these things in her heart.
(NLT)

On that journey to and from the Passover Feast, Mary, Joseph, and
Jesus traveled in a large group. Together. Maybe Israelites traveled together for safety. Maybe for camaraderie. Maybe it was their custom.
Whatever the reason, they went together. And as they traveled, they
sang.

Like the lyrics to a Christmas song you've heard since you were
young, all the words to the fifteen Songs of Ascents were known to the
Israelites because they sang them year after year. The songs reminded
them to go back home and dwell with the Lord. These psalms were
the ultimate road-trip playlist. Because Israelites ascended to Jerusalem, they were known as the Songs of Ascents. And because the Israelites made frequent pilgrimages for their sacred festivals, they're also
known as the Pilgrim Psalms.

These familiar songs helped the Israelites remember where they
came from and how the Lord had blessed them. They worshipped with
three specific types of Pilgrim Psalms. During the beginning of the
journey, their songs encouraged them to leave evil behind. Throughout the middle of the journey, particular psalms reminded them to
submit their lives to the Lord. And at the end of the journey, their
songs helped them get ready to meet with God.[3]

Imagine what it would've been like to sing the truths of these
psalms, especially Psalms 127–28, with your family as you journeyed
to Jerusalem. Aside from the large amount of praise to the Lord,
there'd be an encouraging reminder that your life was of great worth.
If you were a child on that journey, you would be reminded that you
were a reward and blessing; and if you were a young parent, that your
children were a good gift from the Lord. And no matter who you
were, you would be reminded that there's blessing when you fear the

Lord and walk in his ways; you'd sing the memorized lyrics about your hard work being worth it.

> ## Tension Tamer
>
> **What biblical truths do you need to keep in mind about motherhood? About your children? What can you do to remind yourself regularly about these truths?**

In contrast to the shallow words we sing each December about sleigh bells ringing and walking in a winter wonderland, the Israelites were regularly reminded of the truth about the Lord's provision, favor, and blessing. These psalms included powerful lyrics that instilled and reminded the listeners of truth.

In addition to the encouragement, the Songs of Ascents give us another important truth to remember: We're all on a journey. In Christ, we're all pilgrims. We're just passing through this life. As Ephesians 2:19 tells us, "You are no longer strangers and aliens, but you are fellow citizens with the saints and members of the household of God." If we feel more and more out of place in this world, like we're just not at home here, it's because we're not. If we're in Christ, this world is not our home! We're pilgrims. As such, we can find comfort in the Pilgrim Psalms.

In his book *A Long Obedience in the Same Direction*, Eugene Peterson examined what a life of discipleship looks like throughout the Songs of Ascents. "There are no better 'songs for the road' for those who travel the way of faith in Christ. . . . Since many (not all) essential items in Christian discipleship are incorporated in these songs, they provide a way to remember who we are and where we are going. . . . They are songs of transition, brief hymns that provide courage, support and inner direction for getting us to where God is leading us in Christ Jesus."[4]

Courage, support, and a sense of inner direction are desperately needed in a parent's life. As I shared earlier, so often as a mom I find myself frustrated because the reality of raising my children is nothing like I imagined. Current culture is like nothing I've ever experienced. Motherhood is way tougher than I expected. When you pair that with my wild imagination that my kids would have different personalities and traits than they do, every single day I'm faced with the choice to shun or embrace reality. Our daily choice makes a huge difference in our attitudes and in the attitudes of our children.

Yet we can trust that God is leading us somewhere in Christ Jesus. Even through the daily tensions of parenting, there is a good purpose both for our young children and for us.

Chapter 6

Older Children

"You never spend any time with me."

What in the world was my preteen son talking about? Immediately, feelings of mom guilt flooded my heart as I wondered how I could have neglected him.

For a while, I bought into my son's grief. I took his complaints seriously, felt horrible, and tried to figure out how I could be more attentive. But after the initial wave of guilt passed, I stopped myself to really consider his bold claims. He might have *felt* like I wasn't spending time with him, but after years of homeschooling, I knew I was spending nearly every waking hour with both of my children.

Since he was a boy who loved quality time and craved the attention of an audience of any size, I realized that he didn't truly mean that I neglected to spend time with him. Rather, he meant that the time I *did* spend with him was centered around things he'd rather not do, like schoolwork or chores around the house. Was I a mom who dropped everything to run outside and rebound the basketball for my active boy? Not so much. Did I want to sit around and watch movies with him? Not on most days when my to-do list beckoned. No matter how much I tried to give my children an unforgettable childhood, they only seemed to notice that I wasn't spending time building our one-on-one relationships through fun activities of their choosing.

It was then I knew that even if that was his perspective, his accusations weren't exactly accurate. For years he and his sister had been my focus, whether or not they felt it. Our education choice determined much more than where or how my children would be educated; it also meant I closed the door on much of my own freedom, including time to myself. Since I'd adjusted my thinking to accept and eventually appreciate this togetherness, the reality was I spent many hours every day with both my son and daughter.

As parents, it's important to keep in mind that our kids will have impossible expectations sometimes. The key is using discernment to respond to their demands. Thoughtfully consider their perspectives, but don't forget to explore the bigger picture. Once you think they're old enough, have an honest discussion with your children about their expectations for you, your home, and themselves. Then talk through your own thoughts. Bring the kids into the discussion about caring for your home, but remember not to placate them. Choose to obey and honor the Lord as a family. Acknowledge that righteous living trumps a perfect house. As Psalm 128:1 says, "Blessed are all who fear the LORD, who walk in obedience to him" (NIV).

Your children may blatantly seek more of your time, but ironically so often your time is taken up managing *their* messes. The more people who live in your home, the more stuff your family accumulates—and it all requires care. All that responsibility can add a tremendous amount of tension.

Tension Tamer

Next time your home looks like a wreck and you're ready to scold or nag your kids about helping around the house, stop yourself and try this solution:

- Take some time doing what your kids love, even if it's just for fifteen minutes.
- When your fun time wraps up, offer to help clean up whatever you just spent time doing together.
- After the team cleanup, kindly ask your child to do the chore you originally assigned.

At this point, hopefully both you and your children can feel more relaxed and agreeable. You may feel less irritable, and your children may feel less pestered. (In fact, if doing chores involves getting some one-on-one time with you, they might even start asking if they can do them! A mom can dream, can't she?)

By creating an atmosphere in your home that promotes togetherness, you'll keep your focus where it rightfully should be: *on your relationship.*

Attempting to find balance—keeping up with a home that's continually spiraling into messiness yet also setting aside family time—can be brutal and seemingly impossible. There's no sugarcoating this reality. However, not many good, worthwhile things come easily. As a mom who has tried to navigate the pressures of caring for my home and family while also living my life, I've found a few solutions that work well that I'd love to share with you.

Deciding on Your Nonnegotiable Daily Chores

One approach to caring for a home, especially when juggling a family, is to create some sort of a routine that works for you. Personally, I have a love-hate relationship with *strict* routines. After a lot of (failed) attempts, I surrendered to the fact that I'll never be as stringently disciplined as a homemaker who thrives on rigid schedules and perfectly organized cupboards and closets. In the past I tried scheduling every hour of my day in blocks of time, but frankly, that approach was just too structured for my personality; whenever I didn't get something accomplished "on time," my whole day's plans seemed ruined. Since I try to avoid living in defeat every day, relaxing my routine helped me feel like I could accomplish something.

Finding a routine that was the right fit for both me and my family took a while, with a lot of trial and error. As much as I wished it would've happened overnight, that simply wasn't the case. Finally, after considering the quirks in our personalities, our home, and our schedules, I settled on an approach that helped us keep up with our home.

Here's what eventually worked for me: After admitting that what I *wanted* to accomplish in a day wasn't what necessarily *needed* to be done, I created a basic list of what needed to be done every morning, afternoon, and evening. As much as I wanted to deep clean part of my house every week, that goal simply wasn't possible with the busyness of life. And that was okay. Things I could do, however, I named as my nonnegotiable daily chores.

My family didn't need a spotless showplace for a home. What we *did* need were clean dishes and clean laundry, so keeping up with those two chores became nonnegotiables. Also, I found out that a tidy home was much easier to maintain if we cleaned up obvious messes before bedtime each night. Spending some time every day picking up after ourselves before dinner and bedtime became another nonnegotiable daily chore because it was a quick way to keep our home functional.

Because I loosely scheduled these nonnegotiable chores at similar times each day, the work didn't feel overwhelming. If I didn't stick a load of laundry in at exactly 7:00 every morning, my entire day's schedule wasn't thrown off. Rather, if I could get one load of laundry in the washer at some point during the morning, switch it to the dryer at some point during the afternoon, and fold it and put it away at some point before bed, that was a huge victory. As long as I could keep up with a load of laundry each day (two or three if I was exceptionally focused and productive), I avoided soul-sucking towers of dirty laundry saved for one massive laundry day each week. Similar to my approach to laundry, when we cleaned up after ourselves around the house every night, our common living areas didn't get too uncontrollably messy.

When my family did fall into the gentle routine of nonnegotiable daily chores, I could count every day as a win. We made an effort to build our home instead of unintentionally tearing it down, following the wisdom found in Proverbs 14:1: "The wise woman builds her house, but with her own hands the foolish one tears hers down" (NIV). Knowing we were making some sort of daily attempt helped us give each other grace when things didn't look or feel perfect.

Tension Tamer

What are some of your nonnegotiable daily chores? What two or three tasks do you know you need to accomplish every single day?

Getting Your Kids Involved

Right along with focusing on nonnegotiable daily chores, one intentional way I've managed my home as a mom has been getting my kids involved. This has taken a lot of effort, though—years of reminders and numerous attempts. Since parents are instrumental in teaching their children how to take responsibility for their belongings and be part of the family by sharing chores around the house, I knew from the time my children were babies that I wanted them to be involved as they grew. My son and daughter weren't too enthusiastic about starting or completing chores until they were school-age. Because I didn't want to become a nag of a mother, I let their chores slide until they were older. Some moms have amazing success with chore charts and incentives from the time their kids are toddlers, but it didn't seem to be a workable long-term solution for my family.

As I mentioned, once my children were school-age, I started teaching them how to do basic chores around the house. When they were teens and I began working away from our home again, everyone in our family pitched in. I could delegate nonnegotiable daily chores like dishes and laundry, which were both easy to assign and to check for completion.

While each person was responsible for cleaning their own bedrooms, we shared the rest of our household chores as a family. Everyone knew how to do basic cleaning because of the simple yet detailed lessons I'd done beforehand. But once we were on the same page about how to clean, it was easy to check in on the daily chores with simple questions such as, "Did you empty or fill the dishwasher today?" or "Have you switched over the laundry?" or "Did you vacuum the upstairs?"

Whenever there was pushback (like the ever-popular preteen protest "I don't want to do that!"), typically I only needed to give a reminder that because we all live in this house, we all get to pitch in and share the work. If that explanation got even more complaints, I didn't hesitate to remind my kids that none of us truly wanted to do the housework, but we still needed to do it. Cleaning up after ourselves and taking care of where we live is part of life.

Teaching Kids to Clean from the Inside Out

Sometimes you might wonder if cleanliness even matters at all. If we struggle with piling a heavy burden of cleanliness on our kids, should we forget our concern altogether?

Psalms says plenty about cleanliness—but not in the way you might think. You may be surprised to learn *what* we're encouraged to clean. See if you can spy the common denominator in these psalms:

> Who may ascend the mountain of the LORD?
>   Who may stand in his holy place?
> The one who has clean hands and a pure heart,
>   who does not trust in an idol
>   or swear by a false god.
>
> (24:3–4 NIV)

> Create in me a clean heart, O God,
>   and renew a right spirit within me.
>
> (51:10)

> I kept my heart clean
>   and washed my hands in innocence.
>
> (73:13)

Did you notice what these psalms say is important to clean? It's important to focus on cleaning your heart. A heart that's been cleansed and purified is what's pleasing in the Lord's eyes.

When you consider the concept of a clean heart in your own life and in major lessons you need to impart to your children, cleaning your home may end up feeling like a simpler task because you can clearly see the messes and tend to them quickly. After all, it's a lot easier to dust a room in your home than to deal with sin. But don't run away from looking at your heart. While you're at it, teach your children how to examine their own. Through honest discussions, try to help them understand how to be physically, ethically, and morally cleansed from the mess of this world. Focus on cleaning up your heart with the Lord's help too. As you do, your entire outlook on the tensions of tidy and this life will change for the better.

Tension Tamer

What sins do you need to deal with in your own life and confess to the Lord? What sins do you prayerfully and gently need to address in your children's lives?

Laboring for the Harvest

Psalm 128:1–6 is another Song of Ascents, but it gives us a peek into the blessings of a very different parental season than what we saw in Psalm 127:

> Blessed is everyone who fears the LORD,
>> who walks in his ways!
> You shall eat the fruit of the labor of your hands;
>> you shall be blessed, and it shall be well with you.
>
> Your wife will be like a fruitful vine
>> within your house;
> your children will be like olive shoots
>> around your table.
> Behold, thus shall the man be blessed
>> who fears the LORD.
>
> The LORD bless you from Zion!
>> May you see the prosperity of Jerusalem
>> all the days of your life!
> May you see your children's children!

Notice that a life well lived calls for a lot of labor. Because labor takes time and energy, we'll make some real sacrifices—but they'll be good sacrifices! The work may feel hard, tiring, and never-ending. And the work may be truly difficult, stretching us in ways we wouldn't choose for ourselves. But it's worth doing.

The fruit only comes after you've worked. Think about a garden. You do the hard work of preparing the soil and planting the seeds in the spring. You carefully water and weed out unwanted elements throughout the summer. Months afterward, you enjoy the harvest of your hard work. You could never harvest a ripe tomato from seedlings in the spring. Yet with months of nurturing, pinching back suckers, and training the vine so that the plant is well-supported and nourished, that flavorful, juicy fruit brings a lot of satisfaction.

The same goes for parenting. If you want to someday enjoy the fruit of your labor, you'll need to put the work in *now*. You may not feel like getting your hands dirty in the garden of your family, but stick to it. Weed out unwanted attitudes and behaviors. Enrich the soil to nurture your growing olive shoots. Hot, sunny days will come and everything will be going well. Other days you'll face relentless storms and wonder if anything will survive. Keep showing up to do the good, hard work. If we as parents want the fruit, our desire for it—and our working toward it—needs to take precedence.

Picture shoots around the trunk of a well-established, full-grown olive tree. Psalm 128 reminds us that just like shoots sprout up close to their source, children stay close to their parents. That's the beauty of families. These shoots aren't branches connected to the tree. They're independent plants capable of eventually producing shoots of their own.

Like shoots, our children literally grow up around our tables. Once they hit a growth spurt, it looks like they're shooting up in height as they sit around at mealtimes. After my son started high school, some mornings he woke up at least an inch taller than the night before; the extra food and rest at that particular time in his life only fueled his rapid growth. With all that growth happening, kids can seem like bottomless pits. Just when we think we've finished cooking or the dishes are done for the day, there's another plea for food. Psalm 128:3 offers a fantastic reminder that we aren't only imagining this never-ending hunger and growth that happens right before our eyes. Children can and do shoot up overnight.

Also tucked away in this psalm is the blessing of getting to "see your children's children" (verse 6). For parents of young children, you're smack-dab in the middle of loving and teaching your energetic, opinionated children. You're not in the frame of mind to think about grandchildren. But once your children are older, their futures as adults with families of their own become an approaching reality.

As the psalmist notes, after a lifetime of labor, you'll experience reward. After the challenges you've faced and the time and energy you've poured into your family and work and life, all will be well with you. There's fruit from the labor of your hands. There's blessing.

Part of this blessing also specifies that wives will be fruitful in their homes. Imagine reaching a point where you're content to be in your home, getting ready for those children who've shot up like olive shoots to gather around your table for a family meal. This blessing includes the great joy of a family meal. Even when you're tired of meal planning (again), grocery shopping (again), cooking (again), and cleaning up (yet again), family meals are such a gift to both children and adults. Time together around the table gives amazing opportunities for conversations and strengthening relationships.

None of these blessings come automatically, though. They're not guaranteed, and they don't happen overnight. They're a gift in a life well lived. When you spend a lifetime faithfully loving, pouring into your relationships, and working through difficult seasons, you experience a great reward. Maybe you'll discover a change in perspective or maybe blessings will more obviously abound. Either way, your hard work will pay off. The Lord notices all you do, both little and big things, and he may choose to heap blessings upon you. One day, you may be blessed to see the good things that have come out of all your tensions of parenting.

Chapter 7

Spouses

EVER SINCE I was a little girl, I wanted to be married. And for much of my single life, I couldn't wait to find out who my husband might be. What would he look like? How would we get along? What would our common interests be? How would he make me laugh? What would our conversations be like?

In my wondering, I didn't consider whether he would be a neat freak or a mess maker. And I don't think I imagined what kinds of possessions he would bring into our marriage. His character, personality, and looks were what captured my imagination, not his cleanliness or domestic preferences.

When Aaron proposed and we began preparing for our upcoming marriage, creating our bridal registry unexpectedly became a huge issue. As a single, I had imagined it would be great fun to compile a wish list of anything *I'd* like for a home. What I didn't consider, though, was the fact that my fiancé would have his own opinions and styles. Suddenly our differences became magnified. I wanted my home to look just like *I* wanted, but my equally-as-picky husband wanted our home to look just like *he* wanted.

We spent many date nights wandering through store aisles, compromising on how we'd fill our future home. Right away, I got a reality check that as a single woman, I'd become self-centered. I enjoyed being the center of my own universe. But to become a good wife, that self-centeredness would need to change.

Fortunately, many of the choices that were of high importance to Aaron didn't matter much to me, and vice versa. We agreed on the style of drinking glasses and the bright and cheery Fiesta dinnerware of my dreams. However, we spent a ridiculous amount of time scrutinizing sheets, towels, lamps, and the weight, pattern, and finish of silverware. That silverware—more lightweight than my husband preferred and too brushed and rectangular for my taste—ended up being a daily reminder that sometimes compromise may not truly please anyone. After we celebrated our twentieth wedding anniversary, we were given a wonderful gift of new silverware: heavy for my husband's unchanged taste, and shiny with rounded ends for my own.

Houses, decor, and cleaning seem like they might be minor details in marriage, yet when navigating the sometimes-tricky aspects of living with another person, so many particulars can be blown up into huge issues. Just like Aaron and I experienced, the choice of furnishings and decorating styles can become areas of dissension for opinionated husbands and wives. And cleanliness? Opposing preferences can pave the way to inevitable conflict for some couples. If you're already dealing with tensions in marriage, any small but consistent annoyance has an uncanny way of acting like gasoline on a fire.

Appreciating Your Differences

While the idea of marrying someone who could be your personality twin might seem tempting at times (especially when you're in the middle of a disagreement), there's a reason that opposites attract. Being drawn to someone different from you is exciting. Once you're married, however, that initial excitement and intrigue can leave you wondering how in the world you'll navigate your lifelong covenant with someone so unlike yourself.

Even if husbands and wives don't openly air their struggles, disagreements, or personality clashes to other people, every couple encounters disputes. Every marriage requires an adjustment period. (In fact, marriages often face multiple adjustment periods because of inevitable life changes.) Much of this adjustment revolves around recognizing differences, accepting them, then eventually moving on to appreciating them. As awkward as it might be, learning to accept each other's differences can benefit both spouses. Not only can it expand your perspective, but it also helps you become more understanding of others. You and your spouse can use your unique characteristics to smooth out each other's rough edges.

These differences, which can include minor issues regarding your home, may arise because of your own and your spouse's preferences. They may involve the unique ways you think or choose to do things. You or your husband aren't necessarily right *or* wrong. You're just *different.*

Psalm 139 gives a terrific perspective on unique personalities that applies to both wives and husbands. David wrote,

> O LORD, you have searched me and known me!
> You know when I sit down and when I rise up;
>   you discern my thoughts from afar.
> You search out my path and my lying down
>   and are acquainted with all my ways.
> Even before a word is on my tongue,
>   behold, O LORD, you know it altogether.
> You hem me in, behind and before,
>   and lay your hand upon me. . . .
>
> For you formed my inward parts;
>   you knitted me together in my mother's womb.

I praise you, for I am fearfully and wonderfully made.
Wonderful are your works;
>   my soul knows it very well.

>>> (verses 1–5, 13–14)

Just as the Lord is acquainted with all your ways, he's acquainted with every single one of your husband's ways too. He knows your thoughts, words, and deeds. Because he formed you and knit you together, he knows your preferences. After all, he created you with those preferences! And just as he fearfully and wonderfully made you to be unique, he also made your husband in a special, one-of-a-kind way. The differences you have in opinion, personality, and preferences are of no surprise to the Lord; he created each of you with your distinct opinions, personalities, and preferences.

Keeping God's perfect plan and creativity in mind, hopefully you'll appreciate and celebrate the unique pairing of your marriage. No other marriage is like the one that you and your husband share.

Communicating Your Differences

One massive issue a lot of married couples deal with is different habits, especially when it comes to maintaining a home. Sometimes one spouse is a neat freak and the other is a slob. Extreme cleanliness requires a lot of energy, and *not* cleaning and letting things spiral into a mess also takes intention. Pair some polar opposites together, and you have the potential for lifelong conflict. If your husband is tidy and organized and you have a more relaxed idea about cleaning, mentally prepare yourself for some disagreements. Or if you feel like you spend most of your time picking up but your husband could care less about what he does to help out around the house, watch your simmering temper.

How can a mess maker not feel nagged by a neatnik? Is there any way a prim and particular person can motivate a sloppy spouse? One of my friends, a neat and tidy lady, married a pack rat. She keeps some areas of their house neat and clean, and he keeps other spaces filled to the brim with mess. She's joked with him that on the day after he dies, his junk will end up in a dumpster. Yet for the decades they've been married, their personal preferences haven't worn down. She continues to prefer tidiness, he continues to prefer disarray, and somehow they manage to coexist.

While I'd love to say my friend has helped her husband eliminate his messy ways or that he has helped my friend relax and make a mess from time to time, the best lesson I can say I've learned from them is how they don't let their cleanliness or dirtiness undermine their marriage. They realize they're opposites, yet they still love each other and stay committed to their wedding vows. Even on days when it's difficult, they don't let their annoyances destroy their relationship.

One great way to navigate these potentially rocky differences with your spouse is through open communication about your preferences and expectations. With kindness and mutual respect, let each other know what you like.

Author Sheila Wray Gregoire has some great advice to keep in mind as you approach this conversation with your husband:

> Men will be defensive if we try to turn them into copies of us, and reject what is essentially "them." Too often we expect our husbands to act as we would. . . . The best way to reach a solution is to help your husband understand that you need him. When you take charge of everything at home, and especially everything with the children, your husband may feel that he's not needed. . . .
>
> The way we phrase our requests can go a long way in determining whether they will be honored. When asking for help, be brief and be specific. Men generally don't like having to interpret what we want, though women may be very used to

reading between the lines. Being specific helps men to avoid feeling as if they are being attacked. Most men are very sensitive to any perceived "guilt trips," even when we are not intending them.[1]

To help remove tension in your marriage regarding your home and its cleanliness, set aside time to calmly talk through the ways you and your spouse were raised in regard to cleanliness.

- How clean or dirty were the homes you grew up in?
- Who was assigned chores?
- What chores did you have to do?
- What were your favorite chores? Least favorite ones?
- Who was responsible for most of the housework during your childhood?
- How clean or messy was your childhood bedroom?

After you process through the expectations and experiences you both were raised with, keep talking about what you each currently prefer:

- What level of clean do you prefer?
- What is an area of your home you're particular about? What area are you happy to ignore?
- What areas add stress to your lives if they're dirty?
- What are your favorite household chores?
- What specific chores do you dread doing?
- What chores do you prefer to see done in a certain way?
- What do you think your spouse is best at doing around your home?

The point of these conversations is not only to help you figure out and share what's important to you, but also to learn what's important to your spouse. Calmly verbalize your opinions, feelings, and past experiences, and be an active listener to whatever your husband shares. To do that, keep an open mind and a closed mouth. Then work together to combine your strengths. Maybe your husband's least favorite chore is your favorite chore—or vice versa. If so, you can split up the workload in your home accordingly.

Once you figure out what matters to each of you and what you can let slide, put together a game plan. If you're irked when you see dirty dishes in the sink, you can work to make sure that's a high priority chore in your home. If your spouse sleeps better on freshly washed sheets, include frequent sheet changing and laundry as part of your regular household routine. By calmly talking through the issues before you're in the middle of a confrontation or heated debate, you'll be able to reasonably figure out how to manage your family's inevitable housework.

If your husband believes in Christ, you can also take some time to pray together about your challenges and potential solutions. Using the words of Psalm 90:17, together you can ask the Lord:

> Let the favor of the LORD our God be upon us,
>   and establish the work of our hands upon us;
>   yes, establish the work of our hands!

In my home, the cleanliness of floors is a big deal for my husband, yet I turn a blind eye to them and get bothered by cluttered countertops instead. To cater to our personal preferences, my husband regularly vacuums our floors, and I focus on cleaning up cluttered surfaces. We both pitch in with the rest of the housework too, but we make sure our top annoyances get attention. We happen to be similar in the way that a messy house stresses us out, so keeping a reasonably tidy home became a big priority for us.

Looking at the Big Picture

Another vital aspect of cleaning while married is to keep the bigger picture in view. If your spouse chooses to willingly clean something in your home, be grateful for their help and nip any criticism in the bud. Is the cleaning finished? Give a sincere thank-you and silence your inner critic that may be screaming at you to accuse your spouse of not doing things the "right" way.

At times, this feels so much harder than it sounds, but it's a practical way to avoid the truth found in Proverbs 21:9: "Better to live on a corner of the roof than share a house with a quarrelsome wife" (NIV). With basic, repeatable chores I do day after day, it's easy to start believing that *my* way of doing things is the *only* way. But it's not. Dishes can get clean in a variety of arrangements in a dishwasher. Of course, I think I know the easiest positioning to get everything clean. But I need to count someone washing the dishes—besides me!—as a huge win. I don't need to pay attention to where everything was arranged. The same is true with laundry. Most laundry gets clean and remains unruined, even if exposed to washing or drying settings that don't seem optimal or may not be part of my normal method.

My personal philosophy is that unless I want to do all the work in my family's home (and I definitely do *not*), I need to remain silent and grateful when my husband or kids help out. I can thank them for their help, but to criticize their efforts when they're simply trying another method is disrespectful. Granted, if they're doing something that will ruin our belongings, I'll correct them, but I've tried to adjust my thinking to be truly thankful for any help they give around the house. As a result, I can better appreciate the times when I get to clean up and do things my way.

When we make an honest effort to stop finding faults and respect others' preferences—whether with belongings, cleaning styles, or cleaning methods—we're moving closer to the freedom found in Psalm 133:1: "How good and pleasant it is when God's people live together in unity!"

(NIV). Respecting and honoring the practices of others in your home promotes unity. And in a marriage, unity is definitely both good and pleasant! When you make a conscious choice to be united with cooperation, blessing will follow.

Living with an Unequal Delegation

Even when spouses slow down to consider their preferences around the house and talk things over, wives often seem to be the ones who do the most work of caring for the home. When it comes to the tension of tidy, so many wives feel burdened with the compulsion to keep up with housework. In my own family, while both my husband and I prefer a neat home, I'm the one who willingly stays up later at night to complete chores. Fortunately for him and foreign to me, my husband is content to let messes wait until the morning, while I can't fully rest until I know certain tasks are finished. I'm also the one who plans and follows through with deep cleaning each spring and summer, while my husband is happy to not consider a cleaning strategy. I'd think this is just part of my own family's quirky dynamics, except that most of my married friends confide similar stories to me.

Believe it or not, this phenomenon has been the focus of much scientific and sociological research. Studies have shown that many men and women share chores and housekeeping duties in their homes, and men and women both can identify the difference between messy and tidy rooms. However, what science hasn't been able to explain is why men clean for an average of ten minutes a day while women spend an average of eighty minutes a day working around the house.[2]

Reasons for this huge disparity are just speculations. Perhaps women think they'll be judged by other women because of their cleanliness or lack thereof. Maybe they hold themselves to an unspoken, imaginary standard. Maybe women simply enjoy cleaning, or at least enjoy cleaning more than men do. Or perhaps there's another reason sociologists haven't yet deduced.

I can't begin to guess or understand men's motivations or reasoning when it comes to their cleaning habits. And I only dare to take a stab at women's motivations after countless conversations with women in various ages and stages of life. Whatever the reasons others may have, I know what my friends' and my reason is for spending a lot of time caring for our homes: We truly *do* care a lot about our homes.

This disparity between men's and women's cleaning practices could irritate a wife and stir up a lot of comparison and hostility. Personally, when I stopped trying to search for complete fairness in work around my home and simply acknowledged that I actually enjoy keeping things clean, my negativity melted away. Now when my husband helps out, I appreciate it. When I choose to work more around our home, I look at it as something I enjoy instead of drudgery or a punishment—or a competition with my husband.

Similarly, you might be able to ease your own frustration by simply recognizing that you *choose* to clean more often than your spouse. You could take solace in the fact that you're not alone in putting in so much time and effort—women everywhere are doing those things too. You also could consider the promise given in Psalm 62:12: "You reward everyone according to what they have done" (NIV). All the extra work done around your home won't go overlooked. Your heavenly Father has searched you and knows you, and he's acquainted with all your ways, including your propensity to clean. He knows your effort and the way you care for your family and your home. You're doing a good work, and there's reward in that.

Being a Fruitful Vine

In previous chapters, we have seen how the Songs of Ascents reminded children that they were a blessing. But Psalm 128 also has tucked in it a precious truth about the woman of the house:

Blessed is everyone who fears the LORD,

who walks in his ways! . . .
You shall be blessed, and it shall be well with you.

Your wife will be like a fruitful vine
    within your house.

(verses 1–3)

This little gem of a passage reveals a lot about women. First of all, wives are considered blessings from the Lord. As the nineteenth-century preacher Charles Spurgeon noted, "To reach the full of earthly felicity a man must not be alone. A helpmeet was needed in Paradise, and assuredly she is not less necessary out of it. He that findeth a wife findeth a good thing. It is not every man that feareth the Lord who has a wife; but if he has, she shall share in his blessedness and increase it."[3]

Not only are wives a blessing, but wives who are "fruitful" at home are an enormous blessing. What if part of the blessing of a wife's fruitfulness in Psalm 128 has something to do with the way she cares for her family in practical ways? What if there's a greater, deeper reason why you and I choose to invest so much time and energy into our individual homes? Perhaps staying up late to make sure lunches are packed, clothing is washed and dried, and the house is picked up is less about our personal preferences and more about the way God has designed women to bless others through hard work and sincere effort. What if all the effort truly isn't about fussing over a clean home but more about caring for your family with selfless love and kindness?

In Psalm 128:3, the Hebrew definition of the word *fruitful* is to have literally or figuratively borne fruit. Your fruitfulness may include children, but it could also mean the way you're fruitful in your home. Do you care for your home? Do you find ways to stretch your money? Do you feed those within your home, whether they're part of your family or guests? Those are beautiful pictures of fruitfulness. And when you diligently seek to improve the quality of life in your home, you become more and more like a fruitful vine of prosperity.

This picture of blessing and abundant production around our homes may help explain why many women spend so much time, energy, and care in their homes. When we go the extra mile day after day, week after week, we become more and more like fruitful vines, and our homes and families reap the benefits. Not only can we bless our families with our efforts, but we also can establish places we truly enjoy.

Choosing to Do Good

As we seek fruitfulness in our work, keeping the peace at home is a lot easier when we thoughtfully invest time and effort into caring for our homes, even in the middle of disagreements or arguments. Unfortunately, when I'm annoyed or angry with someone in my family, I'm often tempted to leave the house to avoid conflict. But when I choose to stay and work out my frustrations with a little bit of scrubbing and a lot of prayer, or if I choose to stay and cook a favorite meal to boost attitudes and smooth over crankiness, there's a noticeable change in everyone's moods. It's hard to stay angry when someone chooses to treat you with love and respect, even if you're in complete disagreement.

Psalm 37 gives us a couple of friendly reminders to treat others kindly and do what is right, no matter the situation. Verse 3 directs us to "trust in the Lord, and do good; dwell in the land and befriend faithfulness." Later, verse 27 reminds us again to "turn away from evil and do good; so shall you dwell forever."

As we care for our homes and our families, we would be wise to remember that we should trust in the Lord first. Out of that trust and reliance on him, we can choose to do good no matter what happens throughout our day. We can be faithful wives and faithful witnesses to the Lord's good work. And as we trust in him and let him transform our words, actions, and attitudes, we turn away from evil and reflect our relationship with our heavenly Father.

Juggling Housework and Relationships

Unfortunately, as we're striving to be a fruitful vine, we can feel conflicted. One source of tension can involve focusing on getting work done around your home instead of spending time with your husband. If you have the tendency to overwork, it's tempting to get one more thing done instead of taking a break to invest in your relationship in some way. I'm guilty of this all the time. My to-do list seems never-ending, so the more work I can cram into a day (and night), the less I might need to do tomorrow. Yet when tomorrow comes, there's always more work to do.

So how in the world can a woman successfully take care of her home and still invest in her marriage? If your strength and energy are crashing because of the everyday busyness of life, how do you muster up enough thought and energy to do more?

If you're married with any sort of job, hobby, or activity that fills your calendar, and you live in a home, you'll need to figure out how to juggle all these responsibilities and opportunities. (I'll share more tips on juggling in chapter 8.)

One of the first big steps to resolving this issue is to realize you need margin in your life for the sake of your relationships. Recovery programs commonly teach that the first step is admitting you have a problem, and this sage advice can be used in any facet of life, including your home and relationships.

Psalm 127:2 does a fantastic job in calling out the futility of working too much:

> It is in vain that you rise up early
>   and go late to rest,
> eating the bread of anxious toil;
>   for he gives to his beloved sleep.

As hard as this may be to hear, when we busy ourselves around our homes from early in the morning until late at night, it's futile. Do yourself and your marriage a favor and forget about the anxious toil. Invest some time in resting, remembering that the Lord gives to his beloved sleep. Take a break to spend time recharging—not just alone, but with your husband.

Again, this area is a huge weakness for me. I'm driven to stay busy with work, whether it's through paid opportunities or simply the unpaid chores I need to do around my home. Whatever the task, I concentrate on getting it done. In that drive to accomplish things, even if it's something as basic as completing a nonnegotiable chore like washing my family's dirty laundry, I don't prioritize rest. I don't prioritize slowing down to invest in relationships. And while my emphasis on work means our home usually runs smoothly, I know I'm far too much like Martha in Luke 10:38–42:

> As Jesus and his disciples were on their way, he came to a village where a woman named Martha opened her home to him. She had a sister called Mary, who sat at the Lord's feet listening to what he said. But Martha was distracted by all the preparations that had to be made. She came to him and asked, "Lord, don't you care that my sister has left me to do the work by myself? Tell her to help me!"
>
> "Martha, Martha," the Lord answered, "you are worried and upset about many things, but few things are needed—or indeed only one. Mary has chosen what is better, and it will not be taken away from her." (NIV)

Like it did for Martha, making preparations, even if it's good and necessary work, often distracts me. For wives and moms, a lot of preparations need to be made every day. Tasks like household chores and bill paying continually fly across my mental radar. While I'm not typically worried or upset about much, many things vie for my attention. I find myself meeting deadlines and keeping up with housework because they're obvious needs. But my sweet husband, who quietly goes about his days, lets me stay focused on tasks instead of demanding or even asking for my time or attention.

While this sort of focus and productivity might help me stay on top of tasks, where's my investment in our relationship? Why do I let the preparation distract me from what's important? Much like Martha missed out on precious time with Jesus, I allow my own distractions and to-do lists get in the way of something much better: time spent with my husband.

Psalm 89:47–48 (NIV) reminds us,

> Remember how fleeting is my life.
>   For what futility you have created all humanity!
> Who can live and not see death,
>   or who can escape the power of the grave?

My husband and I vowed to love and cherish each other until death do us part, but when death does part us someday, will I regret not spending more time and attention on him? Will I wish we enjoyed more conversations and downtime together?

If our priorities are out of place in our homes and in our marriages, recognizing the issue and admitting the problem is the first step. But then what do we do?

Recalling the Source of Your Pride and Joy

In 1 Thessalonians 2:19–20, Paul wrote to his Thessalonian brothers and sisters in Christ, "After all, what gives us hope and joy, and what will be our proud reward and crown as we stand before our Lord Jesus when he returns? It is you! Yes, you are our pride and joy" (NLT). Considering these verses has been a huge wake-up call for me. Relationships are what I need to spend my time, energy, and attention investing in, which is the same lesson we learn from Martha and Jesus. Even when we're tempted to focus on pressing tasks, we need to consciously choose people over things.

Our relationships are what give us hope and joy, not our possessions. People we nurture, love, and encourage will be our proud reward and crown, not homes that look tidy and put together. At the end of your life, would you rather hear, "I'm so glad you were part of my life. You loved me so well!" or "I will miss coming over and admiring your gorgeous house. No one else could ever decorate like you!" The pride and joy of our lives should be the people most important to us, not the outward appearance or cleanliness of our homes.

Once we wake up to the fact that our relationships need more attention and care than our homes, we can start making changes. As much as you may want a home that looks put together, or as much as your spouse's mess secretly (or not so secretly) irritates you, your marriage is infinitely more important than where you live. A strong relationship with your husband is much more fulfilling than a spic-and-span house. The well-known vows of husbands and wives forming a covenant relationship include a promise to have and to hold, to love and to cherish for better, for worse, for richer, for poorer, in sickness and in health. Though not specifically stated, those vows also imply being faithful in busy times and in leisure, in a spotlessly clean home and in a messy one. Your marriage relationship deserves your investment of time, energy, and love so much more than your home.

Tension Tamer

If you're anything like me and you find it easier to focus on your to-do list instead of the relationships in your life, add a note to your to-do list to "Choose people over things." If you consistently make the conscious choice to prioritize relationships, it will eventually become a habit.

If this area in your marriage could use some work, one wise way to begin changing your priorities is to start a conversation with your husband. Confess that you have a hard time putting your relationship above housework. Be transparent about the weight of responsibilities you feel. Instead of trying to get everything done like Superwoman, let your husband in on your limitations. (Hint: While you may imagine you have superhero powers, he's already quite aware you're fully human!) Many husbands enjoy trying to find solutions to their wives' challenges, so this two-way conversation could be a fantastic investment for both of you.

As you're talking with your husband, ask this open-ended question and prepare yourself, because his answer may not be what you expect: "What's one thing you would love to see when you come home from work each day?" You may think you know what his answer will be, but let him take as much time as he needs to consider your question and answer it on his own. Through his answer, you'll be able to discover one thing you can focus on to help your husband feel at home. The other items on your to-do list won't seem so important or urgent.

His request may be impossible. If one thing he would love to see is a home-cooked meal, but you also work and get home later than him, that's going to be an unfulfilled wish, unless you plan slow-cooker meals for most nights. But while you may not be able to fulfill his answer, you can begin to prioritize what means the most to him. Likewise, you might want to ask yourself the same question, just so you can narrow down the two most important priorities in your daily work around the house.

When I asked Aaron this magic question, he didn't have to spend any time thinking about his answer: He loved walking into a clean home after a long day at work. It didn't matter if supper hadn't been started or we needed to go to a dozen different places that night or the kids' rooms were crammed full with messes—when he walked into a tidy kitchen and living room, he knew that he was home and could relax. The surprising thing was that he'd never asked me to straighten up our house or complained when those rooms were messy. But once I knew his preference and then took a few moments every day to do a quick pick-up, I had an easy, practical way to show him that I love and respect him. Plus, since it made our home look presentable, tidying was a bonus stress reliever for everyone in our home.

Even if you feel like you have a good handle on things, listening to your husband's perspective is vital. Through your conversations, you'll not only understand your husband's one important preference in your home, but you'll also find out some possible ways you might be able to ease your own workload. If he understands your cleaning perspective and your most important preference for your home, the two of you might find ways to divide and conquer all the work a home requires and relieve a lot of tension together.

Chapter 8

Jobs

From the time I was a little girl, I knew hard work and homes went hand in hand. Because my parents chose to move into the shell of a house, my dad finished the entire interior of our family home. For years, each night after he got home from his daytime job, he started working on a household construction project. Whether it was woodworking, tiling, masonry, or stained glass, he took on new hobbies to create a house just like he wanted. While he consistently labored on finishing work, from creating doors to banisters to a fireplace mantle to crown molding, my mom took care of the rest of the housework. I remember needing to do basic weekly chores, and as a teen my chores included summertime deep cleaning as a way to maintain our family home.

Throughout college I only had the responsibilities of caring for my dorm room, attending classes, and studying. But fresh out of college, I started writing for a Christian missions magazine. A year later, I moved into a career as an editor at a daily newspaper where I continued to write and edit full-time. These jobs helped me transition from the carefree life of a student to the reality of working eight hours a day, five days a week, fifty-one weeks out of the year.

As any working woman discovers, I needed to find a way to juggle full-time work with the rest of my life. My downtime on nights and weekends consisted of spending time with family and friends, getting involved in church, reading, trying new hobbies, and doing necessary tasks like grocery shopping, paying bills, and caring for my apartment.

Once I met Aaron, I traded much of my free time for hours spent getting to know him. And when we got engaged, any moment outside of my job was dedicated to preparing for marriage and our wedding day.

After marriage, my free time outside of work hours returned. My new husband, a graduate student during the day, waited tables on most nights and weekends. While we did get to spend some time together, I had a lot of time to myself again, which meant I could easily care for our new home, a modest two-bedroom apartment. For the first and only time in my life, I got caught up on my home projects and personal to-do lists. If you've ever been able to complete everything you wanted to do, you know how satisfying this can feel! The fact that I still had time to spend with friends and family and not feel like I was behind on anything was amazing. But that season of completeness was oh-so-fleeting.

Once Aaron graduated and began working full-time during the day, we finally saw each other consistently again and purchased our first house. Suddenly, home projects loomed and my to-do list grew. When I crossed one task off, two more took its place. Trying to fit in a full-time job, never-ending household chores and projects, and investment in relationships sapped my time and energy. Throw in involvement in church activities, and I was continually on the go.

If you've ever noticed how busy seasons can morph into something even busier, you'll relate to my next drastic life change. When I got pregnant and became a mom, I traded my full-time, outside-of-the-home job for a part-time, work-from-home position, and I entered into a completely new era of busyness and overwhelm. I'd thought I didn't have much time before (and truly, I didn't), but now there was no margin at all. Every moment of my days and nights was filled. Adjusting to this abrupt new reality was eye-opening.

Over the years, my children multiplied from one to two and my jobs and responsibilities changed to online, work-from-home opportunities and an in-person job at church, but life never slowed down or got easier.

The thing is, our jobs may change but that mode of having a million things to do for our families, our homes, and our jobs never changes—in fact it might only intensify over the years.

Opportunities come and go. If you're a parent, your kids will leave your nest, and that will create different relational challenges. You might get work-from-home opportunities or work-away-from-home jobs. You could find yourself switching from part-time to full-time work or vice versa. You might work one job or juggle several. But through all these changes in life, you will continue to face the question, "How in the world am I supposed to take care of my home in the middle of this busyness?"

One of the biggest tensions of tidy that I, my friends, and my blog readers face is when much of our time is spent working but we still need to find time and energy to care for our homes. While we would like our homes to be just so, jobs that bring in much-needed income consume our focus. This tension of working at our jobs while also maintaining our homes can feel suffocating.

How can we find a workable solution for ourselves? Is there a way to tend to our jobs and homes without so much stress and strain?

Figuring Out How to Do It All

When we find ourselves in the frustrating place of trying to figure out how in the world we can manage our homes and our jobs and everything else in life, it's vital that we run to Scripture for help and reassurance. Psalm 18:28–30 brings a lot of comfort and direction:

> For it is you who light my lamp;
>   the LORD my God lightens my darkness.

For by you I can run against a troop,
and by my God I can leap over a wall.
This God—his way is perfect;
the word of the LORD proves true;
he is a shield for all those who take refuge in him.

Feel like you have absolutely no idea where you're going or what you should do next? Just inching your way through day-to-day tasks, almost like you're trying to walk through your home in the middle of the night without stubbing your toe? If you ask him, the Lord your God will illuminate your ways. He leads and guides when it feels like we're stumbling around our life decisions, wondering how we'll manage everything. He lights our lamps and lightens our darkness. When we ask him for help, he'll give it. As David shares in verse 29, God gives power and strength to do what may seem like it should be impossible. David could run against a troop and leap over a wall, all because of God. What figurative walls in our schedules or homes do we need the Lord's strength to leap over? With him we can do it. As we choose to take refuge in him—and not our own strength or power or will—he will protect us like a shield. How do we know this? The word of the Lord proves true.

Finding Creative Solutions

Throughout our lives, you and I will experience many working arrangements. Each new job situation we face can feel a lot like moving to a new home: We need to find creative solutions for each unique set of circumstances.

When we think about searching for a new home, certain aspects are necessary no matter where we live. Each home needs a place to store necessities like clothing, dishes, food, cleaning products, and personal care products. Some homes are filled with cupboards, closets, and shelves that make storage a breeze. If you happen to have ample space in your home, you may have rooms dedicated to specific tasks, like an office or a home gym.

Every home is different, though. You may move from an apartment with an eat-in kitchen to a house with a designated dining room. One home may have a huge linen closet, but the next place you live may only have a small cupboard for linens. There's no way to prepare in advance for what you'll need in each unique home. Instead, you'll have to figure out the best method and fit when the time is right.

Just like moving to a new home requires finding the best way to organize the medicine cabinet or kitchen pantry, taking on each new job—or even additional responsibilities at work—requires flexibility and creativity in figuring out how to manage it with the rest of your life. For example, you might know exactly how you're able to fit in grocery shopping with your current workload and schedule, but if something changes even subtly with your job, you may need to switch your grocery routine around. When one element in your work life changes, it can have a domino effect and cause everything to come tumbling down unless some major adjustments are made.

Sometimes it might take a while to try alternatives and find what's effective for you. Maybe if you're in a busy season of work, you can only keep up with household chores that are absolutely necessary. Or if your job completely shifts, your plan of attack around your home will also need to change significantly.

When it became clear that I needed to obey the Lord and step into a part-time job outside of the home, in a women's ministry position at my church, everything changed in my home as my husband and kids stepped up and began doing much more work to help out. As much as I wanted to continue doing the chores I had spent years mastering, I simply couldn't. My commute sucked up most of the margin I typically spent doing household chores. Everyone ended up pitching in, and we were able to divide and conquer the daily and weekly housework.

One of my friends recognized the seemingly impossible combination of family, work, and home when she was pregnant but knew she would keep working full-time after she became a mom. At the time, she hired a weekly cleaning service, and while this freed up her weekends for more family time, she and her family still needed to pick up the clutter in their house each week before it was professionally cleaned.

No matter if you hire a cleaning service, divide and conquer the work with others in your home, or choose to do the work on your own, you still need to set aside time to manage where you live.

Getting to Be a Good Steward

Instead of focusing on all the time you need to get everything accomplished, one helpful attitude shift is to remember that you *get* to be a good steward of the home the Lord's entrusted to you. This stewardship perspective can rock your world and way of thinking.

After a lifetime of imagining I "needed" to raise my family in a big home (thank you, *Father of the Bride*, for planting a picture of the perfect family home in my brain!), I began to question exactly how much house my husband and I could manage. Of course, we could dream about and save for a sprawling estate on acres of land, and I'm sure we would be very happy living there! However, we recognized our busyness and knew that deep down, neither of us wanted to be saddled with the weight of caring for a large property. I didn't marry a handyman, and as much as I enjoy cooking and cleaning, my husband didn't marry a chef or a maid. We also realized that our life callings often pulled us away from devoting hours to daily responsibilities around the house. If you've ever needed to shut the door on a longtime dream, you're familiar with the bittersweet feeling of logically knowing you're doing what's best but still wanting to entertain the thought of what might have been.

In the end, we knew we needed a home big enough for our family of four to live comfortably but small enough that we could care for it easily, so we bought a bungalow on a half acre of land. Our house is small enough to care for but big enough for us to spread out, inside or outside, when needed. While my kids love to dream about owning bigger homes much like I did, I'm content keeping up with the work in our cozy home. Cleaning is a lot easier to manage when there's less space to clean.

Once you realize certain choices can make your life easier, finding contentment can also be easier. You *get* to live in and steward the unique home the Lord's entrusted to you.

Tension Tamer

As a good steward, how can you best care for your space in the time that you have?

Finding Hope When You're Overwhelmed

While keeping a stewardship mindset can help, it's not a cure-all. When we're busy working in our jobs, realizing we don't have enough time to do all we'd like to do in our homes can still bring frustration. There's no denying the pull of discontentment when we know that we need to take care of homemaking tasks but we also need to head off to work every day, whether we walk across the room to a desk or commute to our workplaces. The issues we face are legitimate. When can we do our simple housework and basic chores? When are we expected to take care of big projects in our homes? When do we have time to work on major tasks like moving, settling in, remodeling, or decluttering?

The struggle is real, because unless we're willing to spend our hard-earned vacation time on housework, we're left to tackle projects in spare moments of downtime. Throw in the natural exhaustion that comes from working hard all day or all night and tending to other life commitments on our days off, and our energy and motivation to work around our homes are pummeled.

Even if we do switch to spending more time at home, our house-keeping issues will not automatically resolve themselves. I thought becoming a stay-at-home mom would free up my time to keep up with my responsibilities, but I failed to consider the demands from babies and young children. Most days it actually was harder to maintain my home because my sweet little mess makers undid my noblest cleaning efforts.

Looking at the Whole Picture

Think about a family photo you've taken. It can be so easy to zero in on something specific. Is everyone smiling? Is someone blinking? Can you see everyone's faces? When we get so fixated on one certain aspect, it can be easy to overlook other parts of the picture, like the really odd way the family dog is sitting in the background. Yet all the little pieces are part of the whole picture.

Similarly, we can bemoan the fact that it's hard to keep up with our homes and work any sort of a job, and we can concentrate on this continual struggle. But it's also wise to take some time to look at the entire picture. Let's step back, zoom our focus out, and fully examine all the pieces that are part of our current situations.

First of all, let's acknowledge the fact that homemaking is work. Some homes require a lot more work than others, based on the size or the overall condition of the home. If you live in a fixer-upper, your home requires a lot more intentional labor than if you had bought a brand-new home. Regardless of the physical state of our homes, whether they're brand-new or centuries old, we all still need to do housework. Unless you've discovered a self-cleaning house, dusting needs done. At some point, windows need washed. We need to clean the floors and toilets and sinks. Maintaining our homes involves work. And that work requires time and energy.

Secondly, the amount of time and energy we have to care for our homes is unique. Just like it's impossible to define every woman's physical home in one description because every home is so different, it's impossible to identify each woman's unique job situation. Caring for your home might be your full-time job, or you might have more work to do in the form of a paid or unpaid job. You might work outside of the home. You might work inside your home. You might work full-time or part-time. Or, you might be busy working full-time *and* part-time. You might leave for work early in the morning and get home late at night, or your workday commute may consist of traveling from your kitchen to your home office.

No matter the unique situations each of us face right now, there is one thing we all have in common: It is always a challenge to live with the amount of work our homes require and the amount of time we have to do it. It can be so difficult to work from home and be surrounded by the messes that are building around you. You can't escape the reality that, in fact, you watch your housework multiply over the course of a day, yet you need to focus on your job and can't tend to the messes. It also can be so difficult to leave your home and head off to work, knowing that the messes that you're leaving will be waiting for you when you get home hours later. And it can be so difficult to spend most of your waking hours working hard, whether it's at home or away from home, then needing to force yourself to continue working as you tend to a much-needed or much-wanted side hustle along with all your housework.

But let's continue to look at the whole picture. Instead of stressing out over our limitations and the amount of work we have, we need to get an accurate idea of what we're facing.

Tension Tamer

Realistically speaking, what kinds of jobs need to be completed in your home every day? How about every week? Every month? Instead of dreaming and adding unrealistic ideals of things you'd like to do in your home, let's stick to a bare minimum. What work does your home absolutely need to run smoothly? How much time will these necessary tasks require?

Next up, let's consider your other non-housework jobs. How much time do these require? How much energy do you usually have when you're done working?

Now think about how much time you have outside of these non-housework jobs. Considering all this, how much time do you realistically have to spend caring for your home? When in your day or week can you reasonably do so? Which of these times are typically your most energetic?

Instead of wishing that our situations would change or we'd suddenly discover a treasure trove of free time, let's accept the truth of what we have. Do we feel limited in our time and energy? That's okay. We can work within those limitations. Are we frustrated because we work from home and are continually faced with reminders of what needs to be done in our home? Are we discouraged because we're so busy working away from home that the last thing we want to do is spend our free time working on housework? Does it feel like all we do is work, work, work?

All the frustration is legitimate. It's all deeply felt. There's no masking the truth that it's difficult. The reality of caring for our homes while working any sort of a job can seem bleak and desperate. At times this reality feels downright hopeless. I wish I could be Mrs. Glass-Is-Overflowing-with-Fullness and tell you that if you just follow a simple three-step process, everything will be better. I can't.

But I *can* offer you a breath of fresh air and a ray of hope: There's relief in sharing your frustration, doubt, and exhaustion with the Lord.

Calling for Help

In Psalm 61, we're given a striking picture of David in the middle of despair. As was typical and quite amazing of David, he didn't sugarcoat his situation or lighten up his appeal to the Lord. David didn't say what he thought the God of all creation might want to hear. He laid out the real details of what he was facing and his raw feelings about them. For example, in verses 1–4 he wrote,

> Hear my cry, O God,
>   listen to my prayer;
> from the end of the earth I call to you
>   when my heart is faint.
> Lead me to the rock
>   that is higher than I,
> for you have been my refuge,
>   a strong tower against the enemy.
>
> Let me dwell in your tent forever!
>   Let me take refuge under the shelter of your wings!

David faced a dangerous situation. When he rightfully could have panicked, he cried out to God instead. His heart was faint, his enemies were in pursuit, and he was in desperate need of a refuge. He needed his Lord's safe shelter. And the Lord listened. He heard David's cries. He was David's strong tower, protecting and providing when the situation seemed impossible.

The good news is that our homemaking issues that fill us with stress probably aren't life-threatening. Most days we're not seeking the safety of shelter and refuge. But feeling desperate or overwhelmed is no laughing matter. Hopefully we won't battle flesh-and-blood enemies like David did, but when we deal with discouragement and despair about projects around our homes, we need to remember they are real feelings brought on by real conflict. Your life may not be in danger, but your peace of mind might teeter in a precarious position.

Do you know who is ready to listen to every one of your thoughts and feelings? Do you know who wants to help when you're feeling overwhelmed? Your heavenly Father.

If you're frustrated to the point of tears or feel tense with thoughts of everything you can't possibly do, pray. Cry out to the Lord with your thoughts and feelings. Let them all pour out.

When your heart feels faint and your mind is spinning with responsibilities and commitments, call out to him for help. He can be your refuge. He can be your strong tower and safe shelter.

Finding the Hidden Blessing of Chores

This may sound laughable, but it took me years of being a wife, mom, and homeowner for the reality to sink in that washing dirty dishes and doing laundry and shopping for groceries would always be a necessity. This is a no-brainer, right? Yet I had tricked myself into thinking if I could just get ahead of the mess and the chores, I'd somehow catch up on everything. In all your experience of dishes, laundry, and groceries, have you ever truly caught up?

When we're knee-deep in work and life responsibilities, home chores can feel like an unwelcome necessity of life. It can be shocking and pretty frustrating to realize they're never-ending. But, after the surprise wore off, somehow I actually felt free. I realized that no matter how hard I might try to get ahead, I'd still have those same jobs waiting for me the next day and the next week. When I accepted that they're a part of every day life, I found that I don't have to think about how to manage the chore—I just do it. And I make progress, completing something each day. Some days, it seems like my nonnegotiable chores are the only things that I get to complete.

As you and I work on our perpetual daily chores, instead of dwelling on the monotony of washing the dishes yet again, what if we use the time to relax or process some weighty life issues? We can sing a psalm or praise song like David in Psalm 34:1–3:

> I will bless the LORD at all times;
>   his praise shall continually be in my mouth.
> My soul makes its boast in the LORD;
>   let the humble hear and be glad.
> Oh, magnify the LORD with me,
>   and let us exalt his name together!

When your mind starts racing as you're in the middle of your chores, take time to pray about what's dominating your thoughts. Pray through work decisions while you're folding the laundry. Thank God for a success from your workday while you're cooking supper and thinking through all that's happened in your day. Dealing with difficult coworkers or grumpy bosses? Mirror David's words and praise from Psalm 18:17–19:

> He rescued me from my strong enemy
>   and from those who hated me,
>   for they were too mighty for me.
> They confronted me in the day of my calamity,
>   but the LORD was my support.
> He brought me out into a broad place;
>   he rescued me, because he delighted in me.

In seasons of life when we're struggling with a lot of work stress and conflict, our daily household chores can actually be welcome breaks from navigating everything else. Who would've ever guessed chores could become something we might actually look forward to doing? But by reorienting our attention to the Lord, we'll be able to experience relief from the tensions of our jobs competing with our homes.

Busting the Myth of Work-Life Balance

When we work other jobs in addition to homemaking, we undoubtedly experience tension about caring for our homes simply because we're preoccupied with other work. No matter what kinds of jobs we might have—full-time or part-time, working from home or away from home—our time and attention are spread out, away from keeping up with our homes, and that's okay. Our lives aren't all about maintaining our homes. But what can we do with the tension we experience?

Once some sort of home-work-family combination enters the picture, we'll often hear talk about the need to create balance. Let's consider balance, though, like we did in chapter 1. When we try to find balance while we're on a teeter-totter, we need equal weight distribution. If everyday life were a teeter-totter, we'd need to find ways to equalize the things we need to do with the time and energy we have to do it. I don't know about you, but balance is hard enough on a teeter-totter, let alone real life! Every day seems ridiculously out of balance, where I have way more responsibilities and tasks weighing me down than I do time or energy.

Because a work-life balance seems impossible, I prefer to think of juggling as a way to manage everything. If you tried to juggle three balls, you wouldn't hold three balls in your hand all at the same time and call it juggling. When you juggle, you spend time holding on to one ball while there's another in the air. A good juggler gets into a rhythm of shifting the balls; there's a trade-off.

If you've ever watched a juggler perform, you'll notice he or she doesn't watch the objects being juggled. Over the pandemic lockdown, my son taught himself how to juggle and attempted to teach me. Because I kept zeroing in on the balls, my lesson ended in embarrassment. Instead of focusing on every object they're juggling, whether it's two things or ten, skilled jugglers intently concentrate on one focal point in the air, the apex. As they begin to feel the pattern of the tossed objects, the feat of juggling gets easier. Adding in an extra object to juggle, whether it's a tennis ball or bowling pin or sword, doesn't feel impossible anymore.

Most likely you have a lot of things in life that demand your attention. When you attempt to care for your home while also working and pouring into relationships, time seems to move faster and managing your tasks seems unlikely. But remember the key to juggling: Don't try to look at all the balls at once. Keep your focus on the apex, and simply concentrate on one thing at a time.

Instead of attempting to multitask by getting something done around your house while you're trying to pay attention to your kids and fire off an email for work all at the same time, stop. Focus on one area of your life at a time, even if briefly. When you're at your job, concentrate and work. When you invest in relationships, keep those people as your focal point. When you need to respond to texts and emails, take time to get it done. And when it's time to work around your home, hunker down and be productive, whether you have a couple of minutes or hours. Instead of flitting from one thing to the next—packing your kids' lunches while answering work texts and trying to pay the bills—get one thing done. Learn from the skill of juggling: Concentrate on one thing at a time, or you might end up dropping all the balls.

As you improve your focus and stop trying to multitask, you'll subconsciously teach yourself what most deserves your attention. Once an area of life has your full attention, you'll be able to get more done on it in less time, and then you can switch your aim to the next thing. A lot of freedom can be found in concentrating on the people in your life at certain times, and then giving yourself permission to fully dive into your job at others. And once you're done working for the day, you can get so much more done around your home because you'll be free to pore over only that.

Not only will you experience more motivation to complete the task at hand because you're focused on doing it, but you'll also start noticing how much more you actually enjoy the way you're spending your time. By getting rid of the myth of balance and focusing on juggling instead, you'll find some relief from the tension of keeping up with both your home and your job.

Chapter 9

Life Chaos

ON A MARCH afternoon exactly two weeks after the COVID-19 pandemic brought the world to a grinding halt, I was outside with my kids, soaking up the spring sunshine. When I decided to head inside to grab a jacket, I stopped in my tracks. What was that noise? Why did it sound like Niagara Falls had relocated to my bathroom? Did one of my children forget to turn off the shower?

I walked into the bathroom and found that all the faucets were turned off and the toilet wasn't running. So where was this loud sound of rushing water coming from?

I ran downstairs, and the first step I took into our basement gave everything away. Water was everywhere. I peeked inside our storage room and discovered water shooting out of our hot water tank like a geyser. Unbeknownst to our family, our hot water tank had exploded and flooded our entire finished basement with at least six inches of water. Since this home was new to us, I had no idea where the water shutoff valve was located.

In a panic, I drove around our neighborhood to find my husband, who was walking our dog. When we got home, he ran inside, turned off the water, and calmly told me to call our insurance agency. Then he began to bail out water—to no avail. My head was spinning as I tried to mentally process this unexpected disaster. Why had this happened? And why had this happened right now?

The insurance agency arranged for a water cleanup company to arrive in several hours and take care of what Aaron and I couldn't. In the meantime, my family tried to rescue anything in the basement that was remotely dry, but most belongings were already completely ruined. Once the restoration team arrived and papers were signed, an army of hardworking men and women paraded in and out of our home for hours, using high-powered suction and fans.

In those moments, what I wanted, maybe more than anything else, was to escape. My kids and I had been feeling sick for days, but since this was before any COVID details or tests were available, we were trapped at home in a quarantine. I didn't want to go to my parents' house and potentially expose them to a strange mystery virus. And because the pandemic had shut down most of the world, we couldn't even check into a hotel. We needed to stay in our home even when half of it was destroyed.

As the night wore on, a heavy disinfectant odor permeated every room and the loud sound of suction droned. Even though our water supply would be turned back on in a few hours, we'd need to wait at least a week for a new water heater because of the pandemic's supply chain issues. My family would have running water, at least, but we'd only have cold water until the replacement was installed.

I felt my whole world crashing in right about then. For years, I'd attempted to create a warm, cozy haven for my family. In the middle of the world's pandemic chaos, our home was our safe, happy place. But what were we supposed to do now? Half our house was absolutely ruined. I felt completely out of place in the one spot I had anticipated I'd find my comfort.

By the time my husband and I crawled into bed hours later, the workers were gone, but it still felt like we were sequestered in a shell of a home. Our kids were camped out with blankets on our bedroom floor along with our family dog, because their bedrooms were so smelly from disinfectant spray. Our entire family was in one room. We were safe but sleepless, thanks to the constant roar of high-powered fans and dehumidifiers coming from the basement. Knowing there was no way to relax in a hot shower the next morning made me want to cry.

As I spent those sleepless hours praying, I was finally hit with this absolute truth: The Lord needed to be my ultimate comfort. Not my home. Not my stuff. Not my health. Not hot running water. Even though it seemed like nearly everything in my home had been stripped away, I had a safe place in God. Just about every one of my earthly comforts was gone, but I still had Jesus.

That night I discovered you and I can cry out to him and know that he listens. We can trust him to provide just what we need, including strength. We can trust him to fill us with his peace. Instead of feeling like all hope is lost in the middle of a crisis, we can remember our one true hope.

Checking the Object of Your Trust

As firm as your personal faith in Christ may be, sometimes you might find yourself trusting in something other than the Lord without even realizing it. Since my family had moved into our bungalow less than a year before the pandemic hit, I'd spent months settling in and trying to create a welcoming home. Establishing comfort at home was my forte. Yet when nearly every shred of comfort was ripped away that night in March, I faced a harsh but undeniable truth: My comfortable home had become a comfortable idol.

Instead of completely depending on the Lord for relief and guidance when the pandemic began, I found joy in being able to hunker down with my husband, son, and daughter in our cozy abode. But much of this comfort morphed into something that took my attention and trust away from Jehovah Jireh, my provider. Here I was, preoccupied with creating a comfy house for my family to enjoy, without considering that I was looking to my house for peace and fulfillment instead of the Lord. When the world turned upside down, I had sought satisfaction in the shelter of my home—until it was snatched away. Exactly how long had I spent my time, resources, and energy on glorifying my home instead of my heavenly Father?

Tension Tamer

When your world turns upside down, where do you look for comfort? What captures most of your time, resources, energy, and passion? Where do you turn for security or significance?

Going with the Flow

As I discovered on that March day in 2020, you never know when life might turn completely upside down. Everything you think you know and depend on can vanish in a moment. When you find yourself facing panic and chaos, it's blatantly clear that you can't guarantee any semblance of order or routine.

Our circumstances can quickly flip into topsy-turvy turbulence, but life still goes on. And unless you're incapacitated, you'll still need to care for yourself, your family, and your home. Whether you feel like caring for your home or not, sometimes you need to keep managing it and family in the middle of life's storms.

So what do you do?

Perhaps a better question is, What *can* you do? How can you manage the normal busyness of life when everything looks and feels like a mess?

While the answer may seem completely distasteful to any Type A personality, one good way to manage life when it's unpredictable and disastrous is to go with the flow.

For years, I thought adults needed to be organized, responsible, and a bit tightly wound. I assumed this was a part I needed to play. Maybe the firstborn in me came to this conclusion? Maybe my born-organized mother influenced this idea? At any rate, once I became a mom and needed to cope with my energetic baby's unpredictable sleep schedule—something no amount of sleep training could alter—my true personality began to shine. (Sometimes life's chaotic circumstances can point us to discoveries we might not otherwise make on our own!) And even though it took me a few years of feeling like a failure, I finally discovered that, unlike anything I'd ever seen modeled, life could go on without a strict schedule (you can read more in chapter 14 about my journey toward discovering this). I wasn't less of a woman, and I wasn't scatterbrained or a failure if not everything went according to plan. In fact, I could actually enjoy life. Like with the feeling of reaching the first week of summer vacation after a long, rigid school year filled with assignments, activities, deadlines, and exams, I hope you've experienced the exhilarating freedom of living life without a stringent structure.

Call it an identity crisis if you will, but when I started rebelling against a life of extreme order, I finally discovered who I could be. I didn't need to be strictly organized. I didn't have to reach for difficult goals for the sole purpose of feeling like I was succeeding in some way. I could go with the flow. I could let the rhythm of a day, even with its unexpected interruptions, dictate what happened instead of marching to the rigid, unrelenting beat of a never-ending drum.

Somewhere in the middle of my complete embrace of the unexpected, my husband and I had a heart-to-heart discussion, and he confessed that my newfound lack of structure and stability freaked him out. Aaron liked the way I used to march our family through the necessary routines of life and said my new haphazard dance was out of character for me. Though I confessed to him that I liked the free-for-all change, I realized that maybe there actually was a lot to be said for my organizational skills as well. I felt like I was maturing into a different person, but maybe, just maybe, I could marry the two approaches. Could I be spontaneous but still have an overarching idea of what needed to be done? Could I still use the personal skills I spent years perfecting but not obsess over them?

It turns out that deep down, I have neither a Type A nor Type B personality. I thought I needed to be Type A as a young, single professional, and I thought I needed to be more Type B to adjust to my role as a stay-at-home mom. I learned plenty of great skills when I tried Type A behavior, and in my attempt at a Type B kind of lifestyle, I honed the ability to shift and adjust. It turns out that those more easygoing qualities are extremely valuable when it comes to caring for your home while navigating a life in chaos.

Even if it feels unnatural for your personality, it's necessary to let go of some ideals when you're facing the raging storms of life. Sometimes survival is what's necessary. You may need to put aside a lot of details and order just to focus on making it through. Hard as it is, relaxing your control *is* possible.

Dealing with Difficulties

When you feel like you're swimming upstream and life is overwhelming, do what needs to be done right now. Nothing more, nothing less. Of course, this isn't a sustainable approach, but for now, you don't have to worry about long-term plans. Because you won't face catastrophe and chaos the rest of your life (Lord willing!), this survival mode is for the short term. The important thing to remember is that doing the next thing is an effective solution to help get you through right *now*.

After the water heater catastrophe, my family spent a long week without hot water. Heating water on a stovetop just to wash dishes by hand or shampoo our hair was inconvenient, for sure. I clearly remember heating up the water for sponge baths and wanting to cry as I missed the luxury of hot running water. But that trial didn't last forever. Though it felt like it dragged on, that challenge eventually ended.

Dealing with our lack of hot water was just one tiny issue we faced. Communicating with our insurance claims department took priority. For days we opened our home at the spur of the moment to meet with disaster remediation specialists. We needed to make necessary phone calls and sign time-sensitive documents. Each weekday during business hours, our priority was what needed to be done next. The rest of life seemed to fall away amid the urgent.

At times it felt like our boxes and boxes of waterlogged belongings would take months to purge. Waiting on the delayed reconstruction materials seemed to take forever. But within six months, our destroyed basement looked brand-new. In fact, our basement was infinitely better than anything we'd had before the watery disaster.

Many times that spring I was brought to my knees to beg the Lord for his mercy. Even in my discomfort and despair, he brought us through the chaos onto a clear path. He restored what had been destroyed. And he generously poured his mercy out.

Without a doubt I can tell you that the Lord works out the promises of Psalm 127. Like I explained in chapter 1, he can and will build the house. My husband and I didn't labor in vain because the Lord did it all. We didn't have to build it in our own strength. And aside from our home insurance deductible, we didn't even have to pay for our dated basement to be remodeled into a brand-new space. Just as the Lord provided far more than my family ever dreamed or asked for, he can do the same for you. As you place your trust fully in him, you can step back and watch him build your house.

Tension Tamer

When you're in the middle of a home emergency, everything feels chaotic. To help minimize stress and confusion, it's helpful to think through some disaster plans ahead of time.

Before the unpredictable happens:

- Make a list of emergency phone numbers. Include your doctors, dentist, and insurance agent, as well as plumbers, electricians, HVAC technicians, and the electric and gas companies.
- Put them in a designated safe place.
- Add these emergency numbers to your phone contacts.

Handing Off the Burdens

When you're facing an onslaught of difficult life situations and emergencies, how can you care for your home? If your house is falling down around you because of a disaster, how can you tend to it?

A fantastic first step? Cry out to our protector and provider. Instead of shouldering the stress on your own, roll your burden onto the Lord. Tell him your fears. Confess your worries and doubts. Pour out your concerns. As you do, remember the great promise found in Psalm 107:1–9:

Oh give thanks to the LORD, for he is good,
for his steadfast love endures forever!
Let the redeemed of the LORD say so,
whom he has redeemed from trouble

and gathered in from the lands,
>   from the east and from the west,
>   from the north and from the south.

Some wandered in desert wastes,
>   finding no way to a city to dwell in;
> hungry and thirsty,
>   their soul fainted within them.
> Then they cried to the LORD in their trouble,
>   and he delivered them from their distress.
> He led them by a straight way
>   till they reached a city to dwell in.
> Let them thank the LORD for his steadfast love,
>   for his wondrous works to the children of man!
> For he satisfies the longing soul,
>   and the hungry soul he fills with good things.

In this psalm we discover so many beautiful truths: The Lord is good, his steadfast love endures forever, he redeems his people from trouble, he gathers his people, he delivers from distress, he leads by a straight way, he satisfies the longing soul, and he fills the hungry with good things. With all that he does for those who trust him and call out to him, we're reassured that we're not alone. He is with us and for us.

Tension Tamer

After you've embraced the truths from Psalm 107, remember you're not alone. Pray to your good, loving Father. Tell him what's weighing you down, and trust him with it. Fight the urge to take everything back and carry the burden again. Resist stewing over your stress. Truly turn your concern over to the Lord. And when you notice you're taking on the weight of worry yet again, confess and give matters back over to him. Even if the process repeats over and over, keep surrendering to your heavenly Father, remembering who he is and what he can do.

Doing the Next Thing

Once you've released your concerns to the Lord and stopped attempting to take your anxiety back, it's time to actually deal with the urgent situation in your home. What absolutely *needs* to be done right now? What's most important? Tend to those things to get the ball rolling. Then shift your focus on what's needed to manage the basics of life. What's the first thing you need to do? If you're reeling after a disaster, is there a phone call that needs to be made, an email that needs to be sent, or some other immediate action? Are your cupboards empty and you desperately need to go grocery shopping? Is your trash overflowing and you need to empty it? It's time to get busy and do what's necessary, fully realizing that if you're in the middle of an emergency, you also have a lot of emotions and unexpected stress to process. Try to create some space to give yourself grace. You don't have to rush, but you do need to do something.

After you tend to your greatest necessities, think about the best thing you could do in your home to bring even a little bit more peace to your mind. What would make you feel a little more safe, organized, or comfortable? For me, sometimes it's as simple as wiping my kitchen counters clean. Other days, you might need to light a candle or slow down with a cup of tea. On days when I feel really stressed by life situations that are out of my control, I take a moment to care for something I can fix. Taking just three to four minutes, I forget about all my troubles and concentrate on cleaning up the messiest spot in my home. I work quickly and know that in less than five minutes one tiny space in my home will look and feel presentable. Identifying something small that I can change and bring order to helps me take a deep breath and find confidence and peace to take on the rest of life's chaos through the Lord's strength.

Whatever you can do to find a quick win, do it, because when you're in the middle of dealing with the unexpected, you need to grab all the low-hanging fruit you can find! It will bolster your confidence and help you experience a sense of accomplishment even when things seem to be falling apart.

Taking Shelter

Whether you're in the middle of a disaster, you've just come out of one by the skin of your teeth, or you're heading into one, there's amazing news: You're not alone. Your heavenly Father sees you in the middle of your darkest days. He hears your cries for help. And he knows how much you can handle on your own and how much you'll require his help.

The psalms are filled with examples of David and the other psalmists crying out to the Lord for help. Psalm 5:1–2 shares a request that's repeated often throughout the psalms, and most likely in our lives too:

> Give ear to my words, O LORD;
>   consider my groaning.
> Give attention to the sound of my cry,
>   my King and my God,
>   for to you do I pray.

Throughout the rest of Psalm 5, David expounded on his request, but it's the final verses of the psalm that are attention-grabbing:

> But let all who take refuge in you rejoice;
>   let them ever sing for joy,
> and spread your protection over them,
>   that those who love your name may exult in you.
> For you bless the righteous, O LORD;
>   you cover him with favor as with a shield.
>   (verses 11–12)

When we're brought to the end of ourselves by the tragedies and unexpected twists of life, we cry out to the Lord. We groan and pray. We beg God to pay attention to our words and requests but so often feel like he's silent. Even when the silence and waiting and wondering feel absolutely draining, we can take refuge in our heavenly Father. And when we do that, we become able to rejoice and sing for joy. When we're in the depths of despair, joy might seem like the farthest thing from us. Yet God spreads his protection over his children. When we seek refuge in him and him alone, he not only protects us but also blesses the righteous and covers them with his favor. That protection, blessing, and favor help us experience joy.

If you're stuck in the middle of a hard place right now, are you seeking him and attempting to make right choices? If so, you'll be able to exult in God even in your trials. You can sing songs of praise when you're deep in a pit. Even if you don't see a way out, you are never alone. Trust that God is working and protecting and guiding, because he is.

No matter how unpredictable and uncertain situations have felt throughout my life, I can say that, without a doubt, the Lord has always faithfully provided and protected. He may not have always led me where I was comfortable going, but he's faithfully been my guide. He's been a refuge and safe haven in the storms of life.

With that sort of protection and provision in mind, consider the enormous promises tucked into Psalm 68:4–6:

> Sing to God, sing praises to his name;
>   lift up a song to him who rides through the deserts;
> his name is the LORD;
>   exult before him!
> Father of the fatherless and protector of widows
>   is God in his holy habitation.
> God settles the solitary in a home;
>   he leads out the prisoners to prosperity,
>   but the rebellious dwell in a parched land.

Again, we're reminded to praise the Lord, and we're reminded of his provision and protection. He is Father of the fatherless. He protects widows who've lost the protection of their husbands. No matter what kind of situation that's brought by loss or chaos, God will intervene. He'll create safe places in the midst of stress.

Not only do we get the reassurance that God steps in to protect and provide for those who have experienced huge losses, but we also receive a reminder that homes are important. They're important to us as humans, and they're important to the Lord. How do we know they're important? Because "God settles the solitary in a home" (verse 6). He knows the calming, restorative power a home can bring.

He could choose another way to nurture and provide, but his grace-filled solution for people who have lost close relationships is to settle them in *homes*.

Dwelling in a home is important. Homes help us feel like we belong—like we're connected to a place and sheltered. Loneliness hurts, whether you're solitary, fatherless, a widow, or widower. Yet God wants to give people a comforting antidote to loneliness.

During my years as a single woman, I was so grateful for the families that welcomed me into their homes during mealtimes. Some adopted me as part of their family when I was living in Virginia and far from my own family in Ohio. Others invited me over for lunch after church on

Sundays. I was lonely living by myself, and for the few hours I spent in those homes, I didn't feel alone. My visits filled me with hope that someday God might answer my prayers and bless me with a family of my own.

And when God did answer my prayers for marriage, children, and a home, I made sure my family welcomed people in. Widows, widowers, orphans, and singles all made our family mealtimes more meaningful. Initially, some of the invitations felt a little uncomfortable to make, but I eventually realized that those mealtimes and visits added more to my family than I ever could've imagined. Those special times sharing our dinner table gave our family precious memories, and hopefully did the same for the people we invited.

As we intentionally open our homes to others who might be facing loneliness or disasters, we can reflect God's faithful presence to them. After all, no one should face life's chaos alone. And when we've experienced God's mercy and provision and made it through to the other side of life's battles, we will be stronger and better able to help those facing storms of their own. As a result, we can help others make it through the tension of life chaos with the unshakable grace of God.

Chapter 10

Busyness

LIKE THE BASIC premise of the movie *Yes Man*, I've found that forcing myself out of my comfort zone can lead to fantastic memories. Be an extra in a movie? Yes! Though I felt completely out of my league, a legendary Oscar-winning costume designer commanded her entourage of stylists to find a different outfit and hairstyle for me because "she needs to be . . . *sassy*!" No stranger had ever told me that I was sassy before—but this costume designer did, and I wore an unforgettable costume for days of filming. Drive on a racetrack for a newspaper story? (Gulp.) Yes! I was terrified to share the track with skilled drivers going well over one hundred miles per hour, but I did what I never thought I could do and turned into a speed racer for a day.

After years of intentionally choosing to attempt more than I might feel comfortable doing, I've discovered that, in fact, I actually enjoy life more when I venture out and do what seems to go against my normal tendencies. Unfortunately, as a result, I typically do much more than my schedule should allow.

Are you at all like me? Do you feel tempted to fit as much as possible into each day? If you struggle with a tendency to overcommit, there's good news: Saying yes to opportunities can result in some pretty unforgettable experiences. However, the bad news about choosing to say yes more than no is that all the living and cramming can result in an overflowing schedule. And that overcommitment and busyness can keep us away from our homes.

Sometimes as we're scheduling way too much, we're well aware of how it will overextend us. Other times busyness has a way of sneaking in and surprising us.

Being Still

When I consider that my life is one that's intentionally set on saying yes and making the most of potential opportunities, it's no wonder that I seem to jump from one season of busy to another. Unless there's a catastrophe, the busyness rarely slows down. The big question, then, is, If we have full schedules, how in the world can we keep up with our homes and manage the tension of tidy when we're in the middle of life's busyness?

Management of a wonky, busy life gets easier through the help of the Lord. Praying helps release stress as we pour out our concerns and potential decisions to our heavenly Father. Instead of reacting to unexpected situations in a frazzled frame of mind, we can live more like Christ and follow his example in moments that stretch us. And the Holy Spirit can help lead, guide, and comfort us.

One verse that I love to keep in mind is Psalm 46:10: "Be still, and know that I am God." As I was thrift shopping one day, I was thrilled to find two simple but lovely framed canvases on sale. One says, "Be Still," and the other says, "And Know." Aaron hung them in our bedroom, and on mornings when I wake up and think of all I need to try to fit into my day, I look at those words and remember the truth of Psalm 46:10.

As nice as it is to wake up in the morning and be reminded that I can stop my striving and know that he is God, there's so much more to Psalm 46 than a simple encouragement to help twenty-first-century Christians quiet down, trust God, and navigate busy lives. It's important to take this verse in context by reading and considering the entirety of Psalm 46.

The Sons of Korah began with a reminder that "God is our refuge and strength, an ever-present help in trouble" (NIV). This, like verse 10, is another oft-quoted verse. But what's the significance of God's ever-present help and strength? Read the rest of Psalm 46, and you'll find out that he's our refuge even when the earth gives way and the mountains fall into the heart of the sea (see verse 2). When waters roar and foam and the mountains quake with their surging (see verse 3). When nations are in uproar and kingdoms fall (see verse 6). When God brings desolations on the earth (see verse 8). Even in the middle of extreme calamity and the terror of natural disasters and wars and desolation, God is in control. He's a strong and certain refuge in the middle of any kind of disaster. And as this turmoil rages, we're told to be still and know that he is our refuge. He is our strength. He is our ever-present help in the middle of unthinkable angst and danger.

Being still and knowing that he is God, our help and strength, will get us through any day, whether we're overscheduled or feel like we're drowning in awful news and sorrow. We can willfully choose to "be still." We can know that he is God and cease our striving. We can know that he is God and relax. We can know that he is God and let go of whatever weighs us down.

While the first part of Psalm 46:10 is well-known, the lesser-known second half of the verse is also vital to remember. It declares, "I will be exalted among the nations, I will be exalted in the earth!" No matter what happens in our lives or around us, God will be exalted. He is with us, and he is our fortress not only in our busyness but also when it seems like everything in this world is falling apart.

Saying Yes Even in the Mess

Several years ago, my family had a completely unexpected and jam-packed start to summer when we moved into a new house, sold our old house, and went on vacation, all over the course of three weeks. Those twenty short days felt like an emotional roller coaster as we found ourselves excited about our new house, sad to leave our old neighbors, overwhelmed with the details involved with moving a household, and relieved by a fun family vacation.

A couple of days after vacation, when I was finally ready to dig in and start unpacking our houseful of boxes, my son noticed that the Fourth of July was quickly coming up. Not excited about the prospect of spending our holiday unpacking, he asked if we could celebrate by hosting a party.

At the time, hosting was the absolute last thing I wanted to add to our already-filled schedule. How in the world could I unpack in our new home, completely move the rest of our belongings out of our old house in time for our closing date, shuttle my kids to summer practices and events, *and* think about entertaining guests?

But on the day my family moved into our new home, we'd specifically prayed the Lord would use it for his glory and bring people for us to bless. When my son asked to have people over, he looked past all the towering boxes and wanted to get the hospitality started by inviting people to celebrate with what God had provided for us.

Even though I felt overwhelmed by the prospect of settling into our new neighborhood and all the unpacking, I said yes. We invited my aunts, uncles, and cousins and hosted a big potluck. Although our kitchen was unpacked and some of our furniture was arranged, our garage and basement were stacked floor to ceiling with boxes that contained the rest of our belongings. I remember the astonished looks of family members as they walked past all the unpacked boxes in our garage. Absolutely nothing about the day was picture-perfect, but the food was good and the conversations and laughter were even better. We found sweetness in the midst of stress and peace in the midst of unpacking.

On that day, even when our home was in shambles and there was no quick, easy end in sight, I learned a huge lesson. My eleven-year-old taught me that life never stops moving forward. Making people a high priority and setting aside time to make memories can help us move past ideals of prim and proper perfection in order to experience fun and spontaneity.

If you're in a busy, demanding season and your house isn't as clean as you think it needs to be, have people over anyway. You may feel uncomfortable, and you may need to bite your tongue and force yourself to smile instead of grimace, but fight your inner temptation to apologize for the messy spaces in your home.

As Kendra Adachi shares in her book *The Lazy Genius Way*, "If you have people over and apologize for how messy things are, whether it's true or not, you put your guests on their toes and distract from the entire point of inviting them over in the first place: connection. You want to let people in with the hope of becoming friends, not to compare your life with theirs or with how you think your life should be."[1]

Even now, every time guests bypass the front door and walk through my messy garage, I tell myself that maybe I can get things cleaned up before the next time I host. But even so, instead of feeling bothered by that cluttered space, I hope some of my guests will feel at ease when they see that imperfect part of my home. Everyone has messy spaces, after all. I hope that garage might make some people feel more at home; the mess might even make my family a lot more real and relatable than if we had every space neatly organized.

Tension Tamer

My family's love of hospitality has taught me that sometimes it's easier to schedule get-togethers close together. Not only is it easier to keep your house tidy if you've already cleaned for company, but food preparation and groceries become simpler as well, especially if you can plan for similar meals or a basic theme.

For example, I hosted a large dinner party on a Tuesday night, followed by dinner with a friend on Wednesday night, and lunch with family friends on Thursday. My Tuesday dinner party's menu centered around Greek food, so I served a Greek salad for a side dish on Wednesday night and a Greek pasta salad bar for Thursday's lunch. I made only one grocery shopping trip, set aside one slot of time for the food prep, and then enjoyed making quick and easy meals using the same ingredients—looking like I spent way more time and energy than I actually did. (Bonus!)

With some low-key but intentional plans, you can prepare your home and kitchen for anything and anyone.

Preparing for Busy Seasons

So often in life, busyness has a way of coming in the form of opportunities you consciously choose to take on. If you're working on a special project at work, the deadline looms, and you know your time will be filled. If you're planning a wedding, you know that the preparations will keep you busy until the big day comes. If your child has the opportunity to join a travel sports team, you know your nights and weekends will be filled for a specific amount of time.

A couple of months after my family moved and held our Fourth of July get-together, my family had the opportunity to participate in back-to-back professional stage productions. My kids loved acting, and because many productions require young actors to have parent chaperones, live theater provided amazing experiences for our entire family. In the span of six months, my son and daughter ended up being part of three casts. These opportunities involved four to six weeks of rehearsals for each show, along with multiple performances that consumed nights and weekends for an additional month. Once school and the shows were in full swing, my family went from homeschooling in the mornings and early afternoons to rehearsals and performances at the theater in late afternoons, evenings, and weekends. The experiences were great fun and highly rewarding for my kids, but absolutely exhausting for me as a mom. In fact, I remember showering every morning and begging God for endurance and energy to make it through each day.

Because we were constantly busy—from a morning of school to an hour-long drive to the theater to an evening of sitting through rehearsals—free time at home was rare and unpredictable. Before rehearsals for each new show started, I spent a couple of days getting as much deep cleaning done around our house as possible. A particularly unforgiving run of shows began the day after Thanksgiving and lasted until the day before Christmas Eve. At that point, our home truly went on autopilot. Each day I focused on dishes, and when I found a couple of extra moments, I'd switch out a load of laundry, clean up a bathroom, make a meal, or vacuum a room. Was every part of our home ever clean at the very same time? No. But our house was livable, and when the performances ended and my family relaxed over Christmas break, I had a chance to bring things to order again.

During that run of shows, we continued to welcome guests to our home. When out-of-town family came for performances, I'd throw together after-show dinners. A birthday, complete with celebrations, fell in the middle of the run. We even hosted Thanksgiving dinner the day between a final dress rehearsal and an opening night.

Was it my finest hospitality ever? Not even close. But it reminded me of the lesson I learned with my son and the Fourth of July party. You don't need to wait for ideal conditions like a wide-open schedule, plenty of time to make the most amazing meals, or a flawless house; the people you're inviting and investing in don't want some kind of fictional, fanciful world. And if they do, maybe those aren't the relationships you want.

Did the extra gatherings add to our busyness? Of course! But hosting people gave me motivation to clean up my house (at least the kitchen and bathroom) a little bit more and left my home cleaner than if I'd completely ignored it for months at a time with no guests. Sometimes adding to busyness with intentional relationship-building can actually lead to side benefits like a cleaner home and a fuller heart.

Tension Tamer

When you've signed on to something substantial and you're aware that your life is about to enter a busy season, it's a perfect time to assess the state of your home. What are some areas that could use some TLC before your busyness reaches its peak? If the care around your home needs to be on autopilot during your busy time, what do you need to do in your home to prepare for that?

Examining Our Opportunities

As we weigh our responsibilities, we need to keep in mind one important caveat: Make sure our busyness is God-ordained. Are we certain the Lord is opening doors and presenting opportunities for us? Or are we busting down the doors on our own, trying to make our destinies happen?

It's true that the Lord will provide enough time, energy, and sustenance for us to accomplish all he's called us to do. But if we are in the habit of cramming our schedules full of every single possibility just so we're not missing out on anything, it's time to step back. Stop saying yes to commitments just to stay busy. Weigh the options instead. Pray for wisdom. What's undeniably from the Lord? When we're unsure, ask if these opportunities bring glory to him or to ourselves. Is he calling us to specific roles or answering our many prayers? Or are we pursuing these commitments for selfish reasons?

It can be hard to examine our motives. It can be even harder to realize something we might want to pursue doesn't glorify the Lord. And it can sting to realize that he has closed doors for reasons that don't make sense to us.

When we've examined our motives and realized that God has called us into this season of busyness, remember that he doesn't expect us to do all. the. things. all at the same time. If we have a lot on our plates, we need to guard ourselves from gorging on everything at once, figuratively speaking. Resist the temptation to do everything right now. We may have a lot of responsibilities, but it's impossible to give our focus to every single thing all at once.

As Becky Beresford shares in her book, *She Believed HE Could, So She Did*:

> God has made His daughters strong in multiple ways. But what happens when we peek just below the surface of our own efforts? What happens when we look at the inner workings of our hearts as we face the hardships of life head-on?
>
> The answer can be summed up in one sentence: *We find a world of weary women.*
>
> We grow weary from pushing and pulling and prying to make things happen. We feel tired after using every ounce of energy we have to serve those we love. We're exhausted in the depths of our aching bones because we've taken on too much and now we're worn too thin.
>
> It's a tricky business, doing hard things. Many women

come to accept the normalcy of being weary because what we are striving to do is often simultaneously hard and good. Being weary becomes worth it. We were made to do good for the glory of God's kingdom, but should it be at the expense of barely surviving or feeling like we can't breathe? Sometimes we can wear weariness like a badge of honor because weariness proves we are doing all we possibly can. But according to the God of rest, we may be doing hard things in a much harder way.[2]

Remember the principles of juggling from chapter 8? Juggling isn't juggling if every single one of the balls is in the air at the same time, and it's not juggling if we're clutching on to all the balls at once. There's give and take, just like with our commitments and responsibilities in our busy seasons.

Take housework, for example. When we're committed to huge projects at our jobs, we need to spend a lot of time and thought preparing for our deadlines. That's definitely not the ideal time to start a huge decluttering campaign in our homes. Knowing that the work project will require our attention for just a short time, we can let other areas of life slide. The same is true for any other aspect of our lives. If we know one thing will take a lot of attention and time, we should not fool ourselves into thinking we can finish other huge projects at the same time. Something will have to give. We need to concentrate on just one main thing to avoid adding unnecessary pressure to our lives.

Tension Tamer

What projects are vying for your time and attention right now? Which project is most time sensitive? What do you know you need to focus on the most?

Fighting Overwhelming Overcommitment

Maneuvering through seasons of life, I'm the first to admit I tend to overcommit myself without always thinking about the actual time or sacrifice certain obligations will take. This has been a weakness of mine since I was in high school. Part of me doesn't want to miss out on opportunities that may never come around again. Because life is short, I purposely cram a lot of living into my days and choose to say yes. That choice comes at a cost, though. And when I find myself absolutely overwhelmed with everything I need to do, taking the time to do the following two things helps.

First, I stop and pray, confessing my overcommitment to the Lord. I ask for his guidance and help, and I ask him to multiply my time so I can get everything done that he would have me get done. Many days I ask him to multiply my energy too, which is desperately needed.

After I've quieted myself in prayer, I grab some paper and a pen for my second action: doing a brain dump. While it may sound a little ridiculous, getting everything on my mind down on paper is one of my most effective ways to prioritize what needs to be done.

Here's how I do it: On one sheet of paper, I jot down absolutely everything I need to do or want to do. I don't worry about organizing it in any particular way—whenever a responsibility or idea comes to my mind, I get it down on paper. These thoughts can be as simple or as detailed as my brain thinks of them.

After my swirling thoughts are out in front of me, I look them over.

On another sheet of paper, I write down dates. If I have a month's worth of tasks ahead of me, I start by writing down the time frame of the next four weeks. If I'm only planning the week ahead, I write down the days of the upcoming week.

Now that I've written down the days, I consider how much time I need to devote to each of my to-dos, along with the date when I realistically can work on each one. I write the to-dos from the first paper onto the list of days (or weeks) I made on the second paper.

Once I've divvied my tasks into a certain time frame, I look over my list of what I need to accomplish and carefully consider these questions: Can I reasonably get everything done in the time I've allotted? Or am I trying to squeeze too much into each day? Are my weeks crammed full of too many plans and goals? Or is everything achievable?

As an overplanner, I always start my day with a large to-do list, but I star the essential items I must accomplish. Everything else is still listed, just in case I get a chance to fit it in during a surprising spare moment. Otherwise, I know I'll need to be content to push it to another day.

For a couple of years, I attempted to use this method with New Year's resolutions. If I could make myself focus on certain goals each month, I could accomplish so much in a year! The problem was that I tried to fit too much into each month. It was laughable how I tried to map out my entire year without giving myself enough freedom to go with the unpredictable flow of life, especially when I attempted this at the beginning of 2020. I can assure you that massive, detailed yearlong plans did not work when extreme flexibility was needed!

What *does* work, though, is sitting down for a brain dump when I'm ready to start a new week or I'm heading into a particularly busy season. For example, a couple of years ago my family's goal was to fill our summertime with guests. We like to host others, and because we have a swimming pool in our back yard, we wanted to share our home during the sweltering dog days of summer. We hoped to invite friends and family to lunch or dinner and swimming at least three times a week in June and July, and while that was an ambitious goal, I felt it would be manageable. I also wanted to enjoy our hosting experience and build relationships instead of feeling exhausted by daily preparations.

Tension Tamer

Feeling like you have a lot to juggle? Try using the practice of a brain dump to get those pesky tasks you

want to remember out of your brain and onto paper:
Write down everything you know you need to do and
want to do, whether it's for the week or the month. No
task is too small or too large.

Once your list is finished, figure out exactly when
you'll tackle everything.

After you get into the practice of turning your brain
dumps into to-do lists, you'll begin to see how accu-
rately you can predict the length of time you'll need
for each task.

The best way to get ready for our summer of fun was to make a brain
dump six weeks before the end of spring. Not only was I able to figure
out a basic summer schedule and hosting availability, but I also had
time to plan out when I could prepare my home for our summer surge.
By Memorial Day weekend, our house was clean inside and out; basic, repeatable menus had been created; and supplies were stocked. I
didn't have to scurry to get everything ready every couple of days because I'd divided all the details into doable daily tasks ahead of time.
Through the help of my brain dump, I was able to simplify preparations and avoid overworking myself.

Did it feel a little bit odd at times to work on chores and cleaning
projects six weeks before we'd actually host guests? Of course. But the
six weeks sped by, and I was able to be productive each day without
feeling stressed.

Getting Focused

Sometimes, when you are in the midst of an extremely busy time of
life with several large commitments, you might feel overwhelmed figuring out how or when you can get everything done. Author Emily P.

Freeman has a liberating take on prioritizing. In her book, *The Next Right Thing*, she writes, "As you simply do the next right thing in front of you—wash the dishes, write the email, read the chapter, have the conversation—pay attention not only to what's happening on the outside but to what is moving on the inside. Look for arrows, not just answers. If God has something to tell you, and you continue to place yourself before him, he won't let you miss it."[3] Simply take the next step, and trust God to guide you.

When we find ourselves overcommitted, it's time to stop and consider what's on our plates and which opportunities we can reasonably pursue with the time we have. Since every yes we give is also a no to something else, it's important to get a good picture of our personal priorities. Which commitments help us work toward our goals? Which ones suck our time? Even if good projects present themselves, let's think through some personal criteria. If the opportunity isn't a good fit with our personal constraints and desires, or if we feel the Lord is shutting a door and leading us elsewhere, say no with confidence. We are the only ones who can guard our time and energy, so make sure we do.

Tension Tamer

Do you have a habit of filling your schedule with every possibility that comes your way? Take a moment to examine your commitments:

- What opportunities are undeniably from the Lord?
- Are any opportunities being pursued for selfish reasons?
- Do your opportunities bring glory to the Lord or yourself?

Finding Precious Pockets of Time

As we're thinking through how to manage housework with a limited amount of time, I'd love to share a trick I call *pockets of time*. They are exactly what they sound like: small amounts of time hidden throughout our days. I use them as a way to still get things done around my home while dodging the overwhelm, even if my schedule looks full. You can use pockets of time as an effective way to crush certain chores.

While some people love devoting a single day of the week to cleaning the house or tackling laundry, I've found that approach to be difficult when I'm busy with many commitments outside the home. Many of us, if we waited until we had a free day to focus on housework, might only clean our houses once or twice a year!

If you don't have much time at home, tackling your housework in pockets of time can be an effective way to complete basic chores. If one morning you notice you're ready earlier than usual, you can take two or three free minutes to clean your bathroom. Simply spray your sink and toilet with a cleaning spray, squirt in some toilet bowl cleaner, and then quickly wipe everything down and scrub out the toilet bowl. Your bathroom will be cleaner—not to mention you'll feel more accomplished! You'll still be on time for the rest of your day, and you just successfully and stealthily used a pocket of time.

Some tasks and chores lend themselves to pockets of time and others don't. For instance, you can't start a deep cleaning project when you have just a few minutes to spare. Remember, this is just a technique for when you want to be more productive in a few moments of downtime. Instead of scrolling through a newsfeed or trying to catch up on emails, you can accomplish something. You'd be surprised at how many small areas in your bathroom or kitchen (like your counters, microwave, sink, or floors) can be cleaned in just a few minutes. By using pockets of time, you'll trade the rare "my entire house is freshly cleaned!" feeling for the satisfaction that your home *is* getting cleaned over time, even with your busy schedule.

Tension Tamer

Think through what you could accomplish around your home using pockets of time:

- What chores could you do, start to finish, in your kitchen in less than five minutes?
- What chores could you do in your bathroom in just a few minutes?

Now that you have some ideas, set your timer for five minutes and try to accomplish just one task. Ready? Set? Go!

Throwing Off Our Burdens

When you're in the middle of the busyness of life, you might find yourself like me, begging the Lord for endurance and energy while you're taking your daily shower. That's okay—even biblical! While surrendering so completely may feel uncomfortable in our self-reliant society, it's better to know that we need the Lord's power and sustenance than to depend on our own. Take Psalm 55, for example. In that psalm, David cried out to the Lord:

> Listen to my prayer, God;
> And do not hide Yourself from my pleading.
> Give Your attention to me and answer me.
>
> (verses 1–2 NASB)

In verse 22, David said something that can be a powerful reminder for us: "Cast your burden upon the LORD and He will sustain you; He will never allow the righteous to be shaken" (NASB).

That verse sounds nice for Christians at first glance. We can cast our burdens on the Lord, and he will sustain us! He won't allow us to be shaken! But if you take a second look and some time to explore the meaning behind the words in this verse, they offer even more comfort and promise.

We're told to cast, throw, hurl, and fling our burdens on the Lord Jehovah, the ever-existing one. Our burdens are things he has given us. They're not haphazard circumstances, but what we've been *given* to face. As we fling these experiences onto him, he is the one who will sustain, support, supply, and nourish. He will never permit those he's declared righteous to be shaken, moved, or overthrown. What a gift! To know that he is the one orchestrating our busyness and then supporting us and supplying all we need through those times? That brings such relief. We can march through our God-ordained busyness knowing that we won't totter or slip. We can do what he's called us to do and break through the tension from busyness because he's at work in us.

Tension Tamer

Instead of looking at your busy seasons as sprints, think of them as marathons. Pace yourself and make steady progress every day. Take a moment to slow down and answer this question: What is the very next thing I need to do? Once you have some direction, put everything else to the side and put your full effort into accomplishing this one thing. You will reach the finish line of this busy season—just ensure that you're not completely out of breath and collapsing when you get there!

Chapter 11

Too Much

No matter how much stuff you have, one thing's for certain: There will be times when the Lord helps you part with something you didn't think you could part with, whether you like it or not.

My family continues to discover things in our seventy-five-year-old bungalow that need to be replaced or updated (like hot water tanks) at the most inopportune times. One unfortunate summer night, we discovered our footer drains and gutters needed to be cleaned out. The dead giveaway was water pouring into our basement's glass block windows. A third of the basement storage room's shelves were set up right under those windows, which suddenly gushed water as if Noah's flood had returned. After my husband, kids, and I mopped up the floor, we noticed that quite a lot of rainwater had poured into the boxes on those storage shelves. The next day, I emptied each storage tote and discovered what had miraculously stayed dry and what had not. Whatever had unfortunately been damaged by the water went straight to the trash can. Many of our craft supplies were wrecked. A few books were waterlogged and destroyed. But what hurt the most was looking through our Christmas decorations and finding many meaningful ornaments destroyed forever.

What flooded? Our basement. And what do people typically keep in basements? Extra belongings they don't have room to keep anywhere else. All the extras I'd stored away ended up getting ruined. As heart-wrenching as that cleanup effort was, it reminded me of Jesus's teaching in Matthew 6:19–20: "Do not store up for yourselves treasures on earth, where moth and rust destroy, and where thieves break in and steal. But store up for yourselves treasures in heaven, where neither moth nor rust destroys, and where thieves do not break in or steal" (NASB).

Without realizing it, I'd stored up treasures here on earth in the form of memory-filled Christmas ornaments and mementos. Moth and rust didn't destroy them, but floodwaters certainly did. The fantastic truth was that after I mourned the loss of those treasured items, I realized it all was just stuff. Even if I enjoyed reminiscing when I looked at particular decorations, losing the items didn't mean that my holiday memories were lost. Suddenly, my messy storage room was a lot emptier and a lot less stressful. With fewer belongings, keeping the space clean was easier. And that Christmas, decorating our home was quicker too—just one more benefit when God helped me let go of what I didn't truly need.

Reflecting on Your Need for Storage

How much storage space do you have in your current home? Depending on where you live, you may use some creative places when storing your everyday items. While some homes have ample cupboards, shelves, and closets, other homes require a lot more thought and nontraditional ways to fit belongings into quirky layouts. For example, when Aaron and I were newlyweds, our microscopic first-floor galley kitchen had exactly three cupboards for our dishes and cookware. So our cooking supplies and small appliances ended up on floor-to-ceiling storage shelves in our second-floor spare bedroom. It wasn't ideal kitchen storage for newlyweds who were excited to use their new wedding gifts, and I did a lot of running up and down the stairs to get appliances while I was in the middle of cooking our meals, but it worked.

No matter what the space is like in your home, at times you'll experience tension simply because you own too many belongings. Take my jam-packed basement storage room that the flood forced me to clean out, for example. The shelves were filled with our family's board games, wrapping paper, gift bags and bows, some baskets, extra drinking glasses for large dinner parties, and a box of costumes. One set of storage shelves was filled with our holiday decorations, and another set held craft supplies for my artsy daughter. Add a few plastic totes with future gifts for others and my son's LEGO sets, and that was our storage room.

As much as I appreciate the belongings kept in my storage room, these possessions serve as a reminder that I enjoy shopping, especially bargain shopping (as I shared in chapter 2). If I'm not careful to practice self-control, the ease of mindlessly buying a fantastic deal that I *might* use someday takes over. But how soon will my deals end up in the storage room?

Part of the tension that enters my mind when I'm in my storage room stems from the question of how much money I could've saved if I hadn't caved in to those bargains. At times my storage room serves as a painful reminder that too much stuff is too much.

Just because my local Goodwill has adorable teapots that would look fantastic in my dining room cabinet doesn't mean I need to add anything to my collection. It doesn't matter if I spy bows on clearance after Christmas, because I can finish using the bows I already own. And I can say no to buying used paperback books for fifty cents apiece because I could just as easily borrow them from the library. Things are just things. The brief discomfort of saying no to a purchase will be far easier to bear than the long-term job of storing and caring for all those things.

Have you ever stopped to think about the ways that the excess in our storage areas ends up weighing us down? Depending on the size of your home and your storage options, you may need to store essential items. But I know I'm not alone with owning more possessions than I truly need. You might be able to relate to some of the challenges my friend Kelly shared about how much tension her belongings create: "What stresses me out at home is all the stuff! I love to shop and the condition of my closets and cabinets shows the ugly truth. This then leads to 'What do I get rid of and what do I keep?' It's a never-ending cycle. I buy things because I like them, but I'm learning that the more clutter there is, the more out of control I feel."

The fact is, acquiring possessions is a trap for me and countless other women. We fill our physical spaces with too much, and managing our belongings takes time away from other things we'd rather do, including spending time with the people in our lives.

Maximizing with Minimalism

When I take time to cull and organize my storage spaces, I rediscover collections of things I like and use. I'm also reminded that I'm not a minimalist by any stretch of the imagination. Minimalism is popular, for sure, but it isn't necessarily reasonable. For example, if you're an avid crafter, you require a variety of supplies. If you regularly host get-togethers, it makes sense to keep a stash of party supplies on hand. If you have several young children, storing clothing, toys, and baby gear until the baby of the family outgrows them is resourceful and wise. All those extra yet necessary materials need to be stored somewhere.

Even the strictest minimalists admit that each person requires some material possessions, and children add a lot of extra possessions to a home. Professional organizer Marie Kondo made headlines after she became a mom and decided that her practice of keeping only the belongings that spark joy wasn't her priority with children.[1] Part of this practical issue is that ever-growing and developing kids need an ever-growing and developing collection of belongings. Obviously, every person in your home needs clothing that fits. And every person needs tools for basic grooming, even if they're as simple as soap or toothbrushes or towels. The more quickly a person develops, the more quickly those clothing and tools will need to be replenished or changed.

While there's no question that everyone needs material possessions in order to live, many people fall into the trap of acquiring much more than they actually need. If your house is filled to the brim with belongings, all that stuff will make for a messier home. To streamline and simplify your home, part with things you don't really love or need.

So often we hold on to belongings just in case we'll need them. There's a fault in this logic, though, because we forget that by keeping everything, we're burdening ourselves with the need to care for much more. This accumulation of stuff spirals into more work because we naturally pour more time, energy, and thought into maintaining it. But you can free yourself from this weight. How? Learn a lesson from the Israelites as described in Psalm 81:6–7:

> I relieved your shoulder of the burden;
>   your hands were freed from the basket.
> In distress you called, and I delivered you.

The Lord can deliver his people from burdens and bondage. The fantastic news for you is that Pharaoh is not standing in the way, holding you captive. All you need is a willingness to part with your stuff and some time to do the good, hard work. Call to the Lord and watch him deliver you. Do you need to part with some of your belongings? Start praying for the Lord to bring people into your life who truly need what you're planning on downsizing.

After you free yourself from the clutches of your stuff, you'll have less to manage and maintain, which will give you more free time. As you cut back on what's in your home and simplify your cleaning responsibilities, you'll reduce the tension of keeping a tidy home, which will then release you to be able to concentrate on other aspects of life.

Leaving Your Treasures Behind

As an adult I've become a fan of secondhand treasures, and while I usually frequent thrift stores, I've also had a lot of fun searching out estate and tag sales. Typically held in upscale neighborhoods near where I live in Ohio, tag sales give buyers the chance to walk into a fully furnished home, see the valuables the occupants have accumulated over a lifetime, and then purchase whatever they'd like. What once would've been a pricey treasure is listed at a fraction of the original cost, just so everything can be sold. Every time I look at the beautiful mahogany end table in my living room, I remember how I bought it at a tag sale for a mere fifteen dollars.

While estate and tag sales provide a good opportunity for shoppers to find unique items at reasonable costs, they bring to mind the ancient Egyptian pyramids. I'm sure pharaohs had great intentions for the afterlife, but now their treasure-filled tombs look meaningless. As the humbling words of Psalm 49:10 (NLT) remind us,

> Those who are wise must finally die,
>   just like the foolish and senseless,
>   leaving all their wealth behind.

Because we all die, we will all lose our possessions here on earth. Stuff stays behind, but you and I will not.

Just like the pharaohs thought they could accumulate wealth only to end up leaving their belongings behind, the former owners of the beautiful estates that now host tag sales filled their homes with valuable objects that are no longer necessary. Since the owners couldn't take their possessions with them, all the objects are left to public scrutiny. And the same goes for us: Once we're dead, our belongings will be sold or given away, and other people will do as they please with our treasures. That beautiful bedroom set you just *had* to have? It might be painted over or sold at a garage sale. Why do so many of us continue to live like Egyptians, fixating on stuff we can't take with us?

Tension Tamer

If you notice that deep down you're trusting in your wealth or boasting in the abundance of your riches, remember this: The world encourages you to believe having the nicest home and best belongings will bring fulfillment, but that's a lie as old as the one the ancient Egyptians believed.

Going from Too Much to Just Enough

No matter if you scour stores or estate sales for bargains or prefer to pay full price for something new, it's far too easy to suspend reality and forget to consider whether something truly is necessary to bring into your home. For many of us, it's probably easier to say yes to more belongings than no.

For others of us, we don't even want what's in our homes and just want to get it out. Sometimes people with good intentions generously pass along items they don't want to keep, but instead of taking their discarded clutter to donation centers, they take it to someone else's home. My own house filled up with hand-me-downs from others once I started homeschooling my two children. Friends and family members went out of their way to give us educational material they wanted off their hands and out of their homes. While generously given, the belongings only added to the tension of *too much* in my home.

Perhaps you're a born minimalist and have a superhero ability to cull clutter every day. Or you might live in a large home with plenty of storage and walk-in closets that easily hold everything you own.

But maybe you have the opposite issue. Perhaps you live in a home that's too small for all you've acquired, and you constantly battle living with too much. Maybe you're busy with your everyday life and have no time to sort through the accumulation in your home.

Whatever your struggle, today's consumerist culture introduces stressors into our lives that people throughout history rarely imagined. Aside from in the homes of the ultrawealthy, excess space and possessions were unheard of for centuries. After World War II, American home sizes averaged around 850 square feet. But fifty years later, home size averages had almost tripled, to 2,260 square feet.[2] During that same fifty-year period, the size of the average American family shrunk.[3] And from 2012 to 2021, with larger houses and smaller families, there was a 924 percent increase in the demand for storage units.[4] Even with a lot more room in homes, storage units have become a necessity for many.

What's the solution? One practical step is deciding to keep only the belongings that will fit into your home. *Decluttering at the Speed of Life* author Dana K. White recommends thinking of your home as a large storage container and each room in your home as smaller containers.[5] Your cupboards and shelves are even smaller ones. When you switch to this mindset, limit yourself to keeping only enough belongings to fit in these storage containers and spaces. If you have more than you can put in a container, get rid of the excess.

Tension Tamer

If you're itching to get rid of your *too much*:

- Choose just one drawer or cupboard in your home. What do you use, need, or love in this cupboard?
- What fits in this particular space? Keep what fits.

- Get what doesn't fit out of your house.
- To make sure you don't hold on to what you've culled, take action right away: Either sell it or donate it to a charity organization.

Choosing What You Love

I'm a huge fan of filling your home with things you love as a way to turn any kind of living space into a refreshing place for yourself.

Part of the reason I surround myself with things I appreciate in my home is because I spent a lot of time surrounded by things I *didn't* like. Memories of my childhood home include a stretch of continual construction projects paired with the harvest-gold, orange, and avocado-green decorating trends of the seventies. As soon as I could pick out my own color palettes and furnishings, I did so, and I've been particular about my surroundings ever since. Even when I was fresh out of college and dependent on hand-me-down furniture to fill my teensy apartments, I made sure my belongings had an intentional style that wasn't from the seventies. If I didn't like the way something looked, it didn't enter my home.

Even today, as I declutter every year, I ask myself and my family what we use, need, or love. We keep those things if we have the room. But when we find things that we don't use, need, or love, we can pare down our belongings and pass them along.

It's okay to be particular about your home. I've lived through feeling both uncomfortable and comfortable with my surroundings. Feeling comfortable in your home can help you experience a lot of peace. The peace from home sweet home will not satisfy you on a soul level like the Lord's peace will, but the way it can make you feel at ease should not be sold short. Thoughtfully choosing what your home looks and feels like can transform a regular house into a haven.

The danger, however, comes when you obsess over your belongings. When you surround yourself with things you love or that, like Marie Kondo describes, "spark joy,"[6] do you find yourself devoted to those things? Do you long to find comfort and fulfillment from your possessions? Do you serve your belongings, or do they serve you?

In his book *Gods at War*, Kyle Idleman addresses how many things in life can become idols. From pleasures like food or entertainment, to powers like success or money, to love of family and self, all sorts of normal things can become false gods we end up worshipping and serving without realizing. Even tasks around our homes have the potential to become idols. As Idleman explains,

> An idol could just as easily be a daily checklist that is completed or a kitchen that always stays clean or a perfectly manicured lawn. Obviously there is nothing wrong with any of these achievements; in fact, these achievements can be acts of worship that glorify God. But when our lives are all about getting things done, we can find that there is not much room for God. Instead, our approach to worshiping God can be checking off a box on our to-do list labeled "Go to church."[7]

Throughout Scripture, it's clear that God is the one true God worthy of worship. Yet it was so easy for people throughout the Bible to worship false gods and sacrifice to idols, and that tendency hasn't disappeared from the human heart. There's a continual struggle over who or what will take the throne of your life.

Idleman describes, "Anything that becomes the purpose or driving force of your life probably points back to idolatry of some kind."[8] Anything. That includes a home you seek to fill with comfort. That includes the upgraded appliances you're working so hard to save for and buy. That includes finding glory in your perfectly cleaned house or placing your trust in a well-thought-out daily schedule you keep religiously.

When we obsess over or adore our comfy, cozy homes, we run the risk of turning our living spaces or belongings into idols. Do we turn to our homes for validation? Do we feel fulfilled once everything is "just so," from the furnishings to keeping things clean? Do we get sucked into a search for bigger and better things in hopes that they will fulfill a longing that only the Lord can fill? Are we worshipping created things instead of our Creator?

Consider what we're reminded of in Psalm 24:3–4 (NIV):

Who may ascend the mountain of the LORD?
    Who may stand in his holy place?
The one who has clean hands and a pure heart,
    who does not trust in an idol
    or swear by a false god.

Are you trusting in an idol? Are you forsaking your relationship with the Lord by idolizing your home, comfort, or convenience?

It's so tempting to adore what we have, but things will only end up stealing our time and robbing our affections from what they should be on: the Lord. Truly, he wants us to find our worth and our rest in him. After all, he instructed it in his Word. But how can we do this when we live in a world filled with so many distractions?

Instead of obsessing over or idolizing our comfort or possessions, let's do something daring and choose to forget about them. Let's decide to turn away from the meaningless things that keep us from focusing on the Lord. We can ask our heavenly Father to help us learn how to be grateful for the blessings, both physical and spiritual, that he has given us and not be greedy for more.

Finding Freedom

Maybe you are in hot pursuit of creating an ideal home. Yet spending countless hours and way too much money on establishing, furnishing, and maintaining our residences reveals a crystal-clear picture of our perspectives. If we hold our homes in such high regard, or if we revere where we live, we've fallen into a trap—spending our time, money, and affections on something that's not eternal, necessary, or worthy of our praise.

How do we get out of this trap?

Psalm 106 provides a rescue through an interesting pattern of prayer and praise. The psalmist began with praise, then thanked God for his blessings. He remembered the Lord's deeds, then in verse 4 requested, "Remember me, O Lord, when you show favor to your people; help me when you save them." After he asked to be remembered with favor, he spent most of Psalm 106 repenting for the Israelites. And what was one of their many sins? Verse 36 tells the simple truth: "They served their idols, which became a snare to them."

Idols became a snare to the Israelites. They also have a way of sneaking in and stealing the service you and I could give to the Lord. To prevent that, let's pay attention to the psalmist's example and imitate it. After confessing the idolatry, the psalmist spoke of the Lord's discipline and then the Lord's kindness. He pleaded for salvation and ended with blessing and praise. This psalmist's action of recognizing the snare of idols, then repenting from serving them, is what we should emulate. Beg your heavenly Father to save you from idols, just as the psalmist did on behalf of the Israelites:

> Save us, O Lord our God,
>   and gather us from among the nations,
> that we may give thanks to your holy name
>   and glory in your praise.
>
> (verse 47)

Then bless the Lord's name in praise.

Idolatry is a matter of the heart, and it's between each of us and the

Lord. The things that creep into my life and crawl onto the throne of my heart are not the same things that creep and crawl into yours. But we all deal with the same root issue. This tendency to worship something other than the Lord is spelled out throughout Scripture, so it's nothing new.

The ruthless truth about idolatry is that the Lord won't sit by and allow his children to be led astray. Through my family's hot water tank disaster during the pandemic, I discovered that just when I was ready to depend on the comfort and satisfaction I mistakenly thought I could find in my home, the Lord snatched it away. I was faced with the undeniable truth that when I placed my hope and trust in something other than my heavenly Father, it could be decimated in the blink of an eye. I didn't even recognize my idolatry of my home at first, but I soon realized that my home was absolutely worthless compared to the Lord. I thought my home would bring peace and comfort, but it only introduced disappointment and loss. As Psalm 16:4 says, "The pains of those who have acquired another god will be multiplied" (NASB).

No matter what your snare is, if God is not honored and respected for who he is, he will make the weakness of your idols known. But when you choose to honor and respect him as the Lord Almighty, his lovingkindness and forgiveness are always waiting for you.

Tension Tamer

Since it's not a matter of *if* you struggle with idolatry, but *what* battles for the Lord's place, think about your home and your belongings. Here are some questions to mull over:

- **Do I consider my home and its contents as possessions, or do I elevate them to** unrealistic positions of importance and worth?

- Do I focus my time, attention, and desires on creating more of a shrine to perfection—perfectly clean, perfectly decluttered, perfectly furnished—than a livable home?
- Do I find myself questing after something as a means of achieving a perfect home?
- Do I spend much of my time and energy at home tending to my belongings?
- Do I look to my belongings or my home to bring me comfort?

After deeply exploring these questions, you might find answers hard to swallow. But a repentant heart and mind can be the beginning of beautiful, righteous changes. And they will transform your home into a dwelling place rather than an object of worship.

Speaking the Gospel to Our Hearts

Continuing our exploration of Psalm 106, let's look at the frank description of Israel's sinful choices given there:

> They made a calf in Horeb
>   and worshiped a metal image.
> They exchanged the glory of God
>   for the image of an ox that eats grass.
> They forgot God, their Savior,
>   who had done great things in Egypt,

wondrous works in the land of Ham,
    and awesome deeds by the Red Sea.
Therefore he said he would destroy them—
    had not Moses, his chosen one,
stood in the breach before him,
    to turn away his wrath from destroying them.

(verses 19–23)

If you're tempted to go your own way and leave God out of the picture in our consumeristic, materialistic age, learn from the Israelites' mistakes! Don't turn your home into an idol. Don't exchange the glory of God for the image of cheap belongings in your home. Don't forget God, your Savior.

And if you've already unknowingly embraced these idols, it's not too late to repent. Simply put, repenting means to stop and turn around. If you feel regret for what you've done, then turn from that sin and dedicate yourself to changing your former pattern. Ask the Lord for forgiveness and sincerely ask him for his help in changing your heart, mind, and habits.

As author Dee Brestin explains, "We have such deceitful hearts that we are willing to go back into slavery rather than release our heart idols. Implicit in every temptation is the deception that God doesn't care for us, so we must take matters into our own hands. Again, we must remind our souls that he cares for us. We can speak the gospel to our hearts, and we can also remember the times in the past when he *has* cared for us."[9]

We need to speak the gospel to our hearts. We need to remind our souls of the many ways God cares for us. And we need to understand the warning in Psalm 52, where David shared:

The righteous will see and fear;
    they will laugh at you, saying,

"Here now is the man
   who did not make God his stronghold
but trusted in his great wealth."
(verses 6–7 NIV)

Instead of trusting in the Lord or seeking refuge in him, this man trusted in the abundance of his own riches. Yet verse 5 (NIV) reveals the Lord's response:

Surely God will bring you down to everlasting ruin:
   He will snatch you up and pluck you from your tent;
   he will uproot you from the land of the living.

Imagine devoting your life to acquiring riches and accumulating stuff, fully trusting in all that you see around your home, only to be brought to ruin. Belongings may bring a lot of physical comfort in this world, but there's no way I'd choose a cushy life if it meant being snatched up, plucked out, and uprooted by the Lord. Absolutely no temporary pleasure is worth those consequences.

Fortunately for us, David didn't leave us wondering about the alternative life choice. He spelled out the hope found in right choices:

But I am like an olive tree
   flourishing in the house of God;
I trust in God's unfailing love
   for ever and ever.
For what you have done I will always praise you
   in the presence of your faithful people.
And I will hope in your name,
   for your name is good.
(verses 8–9 NIV)

These comforting verses teach us that when we trust in the Lord's unfailing love, we will flourish in the house of God. Our lives will be filled with praise to the Lord, not praise to our belongings. Our hope can rest in him—rather than in earthly treasures—because his name is good. And as we trust in our heavenly Father and praise his name, we'll flourish like an olive tree.

Maybe you're wondering why in the world you'd want to flourish like an olive tree. Symbolically speaking, olive trees provide a picture of the Lord's anointing, because in biblical times, olives produced the oil that was used for anointing. Also, offered as sacrifices and used to signify peace and comfort, olives represent goodness, blessing, and favor throughout the Bible. What's the goodness, blessing, and favor of the Lord's anointed in Psalm 52? Being chosen to flourish in the house of God.

Every day, you and I have a choice to flourish or flounder. Most likely, if asked, we would say that we want to flourish. Yet how many of us end up making random choices that lead straight to floundering instead? In Psalm 52, David revealed the better way. We can flourish by trusting in God's unfailing love, praising our Father in the presence of other Christians, and hoping in his name.

Easy peasy, lemon squeezy, right? Maybe not. This truth might be easy to understand, but it's difficult to live out. If you tend to feel trapped by the physical and mental weight of all your stuff, or if you tend to idolize your home and all you own, it's time to create some reminders throughout your day.

Schedule check-in moments in your day when it makes the most sense for you (you can even set reminders on your phone), and ask yourself three questions inspired by Psalm 52: First, am I trusting in God and his unfailing love today? Second, how can I praise the Lord right now? And third, how am I hoping in his name?

That's it. Notice there isn't any five-step clutter-busting method or no-spend challenge here. Simply focus on the Lord. Trust him, praise him, and hope in him. As you do that, your idols will come crashing down, and the Lord will begin working in your heart and mind. He'll make it so you'll want to free yourself of whatever tries to stand in his way. As the old hymn reminds us, "Turn your eyes upon Jesus, look full in his wonderful face, and the things of earth will grow strangely dim in the light of His glory and grace."[10]

When we turn our eyes upon Jesus, we'll find freedom from our idols. He can free our hearts, souls, minds, and strength from the tension of too much.

Chapter 12

Discontentment

SOMETIMES IN LIFE, you can feel discontentment brewing like a big storm in your heart and mind. Other times, it smacks you in the face when you least expect it. That's how I felt during the Great Recession of the late 2000s, when my husband shared with me an idea he'd been mulling over regarding our future. "Maybe we're supposed to be like the Israelites who were called away from their homes. Maybe we're supposed to leave, but God will bring us back."

No matter how well-intentioned or biblically based his logic was, I didn't want to listen. I felt content with our life, and I was unwilling to disrupt that peace and happiness, especially since my contentment had come despite odd circumstances. Due to the recession, both Aaron and I had been downsized from our jobs within three months of each other, and we had no job prospects on the horizon. Now seven months into unemployment, we were spending through our savings as we tried to pay our mortgage and the hospital bills we'd incurred from an emergency C-section when our daughter was born. Our finances weren't the only thing dwindling; life with a newborn and a toddler brought sleep and energy deprivation too. Ever the provider, Aaron was set on moving anywhere for potential jobs, but I was convinced we needed to stay in our well-loved home.

At a point when absolutely no job possibilities could be found within an hour's drive of where we lived, Aaron chose to accept a job three hours away—teaching at a maximum-security prison. Because I was still recovering from surgery and postpartum depression, I received this news through a flood of hormones and emotions. Aaron was the recipient of a lot of my anger, drama, and sorrow. He left for job training, and I stayed behind to pack up and clean our home to sell while still taking care of our two babies. I did not want to make this move. I did not want to sell our home.

At the very same time, my beloved grandma was also forced to make a move she didn't want to make. Together we'd talk and cry over our realities, knowing that although we were in completely different seasons of life, we were both experiencing the same desperate, heartbreaking situation. We found out that no matter what kind of pity party we threw for ourselves and no matter how much we opposed the decisions, we were helpless to make any changes.

Whether I liked it or not, my family's house sold exactly forty days after we listed it, and we broke even. We moved into a tiny two-bedroom town house, where we filled our single-car garage floor to ceiling with boxes. Our first home had been modest, for sure, but it still seemed incredibly spacious compared to this tiny place.

Day after day, I woke up in our town house bedroom and thought of how much I disliked where we were. I didn't want to settle into this place where I didn't want to live, so I chose not to decorate. The small windows looked out onto parking lots and other buildings, which only exacerbated my depression. In our old home, located in a friendly neighborhood with tree-lined streets, I'd soaked up every moment of my son's first year of life with plenty of joy and wonder, but in the first year of my daughter's life, I was filled with bitterness. Aaron and I disagreed over almost everything as he tried hard to make our new life work and I was set on reminding us of what we lost. When I developed a huge bleeding ulcer on my lip, I realized it was a visible manifestation of the hostility churning inside of me.

I clearly remember what it felt like to try to entertain my two children each morning even as I was still searching for the motivation to start another day. I'd bring them both to my bedroom in their little onesies and footed pajamas and turn on the soundtrack to *Willy Wonka and the Chocolate Factory*, of all things. As I hurried to get ready in our adjoined bathroom, I'd weep even as I tried to sing along with the cheerfully idyllic lyrics about chocolate, golden tickets, and paradise. The music entertained my sweet babies, but they looked a little puzzled as to why their mommy was crying. I'd hop in the shower and pull myself together, and then we'd move on with our day. We'd typically go out and about for adventures because I wanted to spend as little time in that rental as possible.

We stayed in that town house for fourteen months before experiencing the exodus Aaron had predicted. In fact, the Lord relocated us relatively close to our first home, and we settled in as a family. But for those fourteen months away, I discovered that you can truly hate where you're living. By holding on to bitterness and dwelling on thoughts of what's been lost, it's possible to make yourself sick and overwhelmed with disappointment and discontentment.

Living Where You Don't Want to Live

When you find yourself living in a place you didn't choose, it's tempting to obsess over your disappointment. It's easy to hold grudges, especially when you face circumstances you would never choose for yourself. And it can be heartbreaking to remember what you once were privileged to have but now have left behind.

The Israelites knew this unwelcome upheaval all too well. During the period of Babylonian captivity, they were sent away from their familiar homes and surroundings into a strange new land. Devastated by life as captives in a foreign place, they didn't ever want to forget the promised land they left behind. Psalm 137:1 documents their sorrow:

> By the waters of Babylon,
>> there we sat down and wept,
>> when we remembered Zion.

Their experience shows it's natural to grieve what you've lost.

Blooming where you're planted can be very difficult, especially when you don't approve of where you've been planted. Maybe you're living in a home filled with painful memories from the past. Friends of mine have struggled to move in and start their marriages in homes where their new husbands had previously lived with ex-wives. Or you may live in an unsafe neighborhood, or in a home that is literally falling down around you, but for various reasons you can't move away. If you know you'd rather move on but can't, the thought of investing time, money, or your emotions into settling in to your current location can feel like a waste.

You might feel reassured to know that you don't need to gloss over what you're feeling. You're not required to put on a happy face and pretend that everything is wonderful. You can admit your uncomfortable thoughts and spend time trying to process your situation. But instead of finding yourself stuck dwelling on the negative and letting your complaints and worries keep you down, confess them to the Lord. Talk things over with him.

When David feared for his life and hid from Saul in a cave, he didn't pretend that everything was sunshine and rainbows. He was honest with the Lord. For us, reading his honesty while in the middle of rough circumstances can be comforting. In Psalm 142, David prayed:

> I cry out to the LORD;
>> I plead for the LORD's mercy.

I pour out my complaints before him
>   and tell him all my troubles.
When I am overwhelmed,
>   you alone know the way I should turn.
Wherever I go,
>   my enemies have set traps for me.
I look for someone to come and help me,
>   but no one gives me a passing thought!
No one will help me;
>   no one cares a bit what happens to me.
Then I pray to you, O LORD.
>   I say, "You are my place of refuge.
>   You are all I really want in life.
Hear my cry,
>   for I am very low."

>   (verses 1–6 NLT)

When you're feeling very low, pour out your complaints and tell all your troubles to your heavenly Father. He wants to hear from you; when you're overwhelmed, he cares. You can cry out to him. Most likely your situation won't change in an instant. But he will pour out his comfort and strength so you can continue even in the middle of struggles.

No matter what living situation you find yourself in, you might wrestle with feelings of frustration and discontentment at times. Even in a secure house where you once felt excited to live, perhaps you're frustrated because things have become completely outdated and you're unable to add the updates you'd prefer due to financial constraints. My friend Cindy fights this specific source of discontent in a wise way: "The greatest stress for me is seeing the areas of my home that need to be renovated or remodeled yet knowing I don't have the money to do the work. To help me combat the stress, I keep it clean. I also decorate to camouflage those areas. It's like dressing yourself to accentuate your best physical features."

Even if you're living in the home that you want to live in and you're quite content, you may notice that feelings of discontentment show up every now and then. Maybe it's when you realize your home doesn't look like a designer's masterpiece you'd see on a home improvement show. By sticking with what you already have, you may struggle with feeling like you can't keep up with everyone else.

Maybe you don't have the creativity, artistry, or finances to make things look exactly like you want. You'd love to have a gorgeous, spacious outdoor living space, complete with cushy patio furniture, an outdoor kitchen, and mood lighting, but you only have the resources for a balcony with a couple of folding chairs and a pot of flowers.

Or maybe you're holding back on sharing your home with others because you're not quite happy or confident that you have a "perfect" home. All that displeasure gets in the way of feeling truly content with your current living situation.

Finding Contentment

Whatever your situation, discontentment is a real issue we all deal with. So often, we seek our validation and satisfaction in our homes and belongings. Yet if we keep seeking contentment in our possessions, we'll end up being disappointed.

Contentment has a way of being head knowledge instead of heart knowledge; we know in our minds that contentment is best, yet it's hard to truly feel it or embrace it. We can read Philippians 4:11–13 and understand what the apostle Paul said:

> Actually, I don't have a sense of needing anything personally. I've learned by now to be quite content whatever my circumstances. I'm just as happy with little as with much, with much as with little. I've found the recipe for being happy whether

full or hungry, hands full or hands empty. Whatever I have, wherever I am, I can make it through anything in the One who makes me who I am. (MSG)

Even though our minds may understand and even want to live this way, it's a challenge to truly embrace these words and live them out. True contentment is a difficult lesson to learn deep in our hearts. It can be a hard choice to make.

Contentment is especially hard to come by in our world, where we're bombarded daily with images and messages of acquiring more or seeking happiness in the latest and the greatest. Discontentment is encouraged, because if we were content with exactly what we had in our homes, how could marketers persuade us to spend our hard-earned money? If we've been taught one thing by retailers in the twenty-first century, it's that we should continually quest for bigger and better things to make us happy (as discussed in chapter 2). This popular mindset is completely contrary to the Bible's perspective, though.

Paul's words to the Philippian church about contentment were a mystery the world didn't understand then or now. Yet Paul repeated the same encouragement to seek contentment when he wrote to his friend and son in the faith, Timothy: "Godliness with contentment is great gain. For we brought nothing into the world, and we can take nothing out of it" (1 Timothy 6:6–7 NIV). The author of Hebrews also warned against discontent: "Keep your lives free from the love of money and be content with what you have, because God has said, 'Never will I leave you; never will I forsake you'" (Hebrews 13:5 NIV).

Godly contentment like Paul experienced means finding satisfaction in whatever conditions we find ourselves in. While our modern-day definition of contentment centers around self-sufficiency, believers in Christ get to be Christ-sufficient. We can fully admit that we're not enough, but *he* is enough. Living out the truth that contentment is only possible when we rely on the power of Christ happens when we trust in his sufficiency, not our own.

Is godly contentment foreign to most people? Yes! It *always* has been. From Eve's temptation to want something more in the garden of Eden, to the Israelites' dissatisfaction with God's provision in the wilderness, to our own quest for "better" today, discontentment is a common trait experienced by all humans. When we examine the root of discontentment, we find that it comes from trusting in the things of this world. We're looking to possessions and experiences to help us feel fulfilled instead of finding our fulfillment in Christ. But contentment doesn't depend on our circumstances.

The end of Hebrews 13:5 offers an antidote to discontentment—and it's not at all found in homes or belongings. The solution prescribed is remembering the Lord's presence and provision. We can be content with exactly what we have because the Lord won't leave or forsake us. This is a great reminder that experiencing contentment—or a lack of it—isn't based on our needs. God provides everything we need, even if it's not exactly what we may want, and he will continue to do so. No matter what we may believe, contentment won't be found in getting everything we want.

Finding contentment boils down to finding satisfaction in Christ alone. And that, my friend, is a hard concept to live out day after day in a world that trains you to look everywhere *but* Christ for your enjoyment and peace. Hard concept or not, though, believers in Christ need to grasp it. As Elisabeth Elliot wrote, "A spirit of calm contentment always accompanies true godliness. The deep peace that comes from deep trust in God's lovingkindness is not destroyed even by the worst of circumstances, for those Everlasting Arms are still cradling us."[1]

Trust in God's lovingkindness lies at the center of how we can find contentment with our homes. If we're experiencing a deep, true peace wherever we find ourselves living, it's only because we have a deep trust in our Father and his lovingkindness. And if we're *not* experiencing a deep peace, but rather discontent and doubt, then who or what are we trusting in?

Elliot went on to say, "Everything about which we are tempted to complain may be the very instrument whereby the Potter intends to shape His clay into the image of His Son—a headache, an insult, a long line at the check-out, someone's rudeness or failure to say thank you, misunderstanding, disappointment, interruption."[2]

Most likely the very things in our homes that annoy us are what our Father is using to sanctify us and make us more like himself. We're living the lives the Lord has chosen for us to live, not lives we've chosen for ourselves. As we realize and believe that God controls all things and faithfully provides for all our necessities, we're freed from obsessing over our circumstances.

When our lives or homes look nothing like we hoped or planned, let's try trusting that we'll find satisfaction in the Lord's sovereignty. We may not understand his plans, but we can trust that he is all-knowing and all-powerful. We can find contentment as we surrender our lives to him. On the flip side, if we choose to fight his plan and try to get our own ways, we won't find contentment. And we probably won't end up with the results we were aiming for anyway.

Tension Tamer

If life looks disappointingly different from how you hoped it would, how can you keep the following truths at the forefront of your mind so you can strengthen and comfort yourself with them daily?

- God directs all things toward his divine purpose.
- Your home may not feel perfect, but God is perfect.

- **Through his providence, God controls all things according to his perfect will.**

Longing for Home

Strangely enough, our deeply rooted desires for something better are actually good feelings. They should remind us that we are strangers in this world. We're just passing through. We're meant for more. And we're created to yearn for more. As the Sons of Korah wrote in Psalm 84:1–4:

> How lovely is your dwelling place,
>   O LORD of hosts!
> My soul longs, yes, faints
>   for the courts of the LORD;
> my heart and flesh sing for joy
>   to the living God.
>
> Even the sparrow finds a home,
>   and the swallow a nest for herself,
>   where she may lay her young,
> at your altars, O LORD of hosts,
>   my King and my God.
> Blessed are those who dwell in your house,
>   ever singing your praise!

Did you catch that? Centuries before our desires were shaped by the daily onslaught of advertising, a soul longed, even fainted, for the courts of the Lord. There was deep desire. There was a calling for something more. There was a longing to be with the Lord. We were created to crave our Creator.

In their book *The Sacred Romance*, Brent Curtis and John Eldredge write,

> Someone or something has romanced us from the beginning with creek-side singers and pastel sunsets, with the austere majesty of snow-capped mountains and the poignant flames of autumn colors telling us of something—or someone— leaving, with a promise to return. These things can, in an unguarded moment, bring us to our knees with longing for this something or someone who is lost; someone or something only our heart recognizes. . . . It is as if someone has left us with a haunting in our inner-heart stories that will not go away; nor will it allow itself to be captured and ordered.[3]

This deep longing in our hearts for something more will never be satisfied by a picture-perfect home. Even if you won the lottery, bought the house of your dreams, and filled every room with whatever you've ever wished for, you'd still experience the longing for something more. You'd still seek the goal of contentment. Will those passing fancies make you smile? Probably so. But they won't fill your heart with fullness or completion. True contentment won't happen because of a perfectly clean, beautifully decorated home. That deep-down peace and satisfaction comes through Christ alone.

Max Lucado explains,

> The twists and turns of life have a way of reminding us—we aren't home here. This is not our homeland. We aren't fluent in the languages of disease and death. The culture confuses the heart, the noise disrupts our sleep, and we feel far from home.
>
> And you know what? That's OK. . . .
>
> You have an eternal address fixed in your mind. . . . God

has "set eternity in the hearts of men" (Ecclesiastes 3:11 NIV).
Deep down you know you are not home yet.

So be careful not to act like you are.[4]

When you and I face disappointment and discontentment, it's a perfect opportunity to slow down and remember the ultimate reason we're experiencing longing and searching for something else. We can't find true satisfaction in our homes and lives and plans, but those conflicted and unsettled feelings can lead us to remember that we have been created for so much more. We've been created for an eternity with our Creator.

Watching the Birds

There's a lot more tucked into the first few verses of Psalm 84 than just a deep longing for the Lord. In fact, there's a bit of an object lesson on the secret to contentment. Verse 3 reminds us,

> Even the sparrow finds a home,
>   and the swallow a nest for herself,
>   where she may lay her young,
> at your altars, O LORD of hosts,
>   my King and my God.

What can birds teach us about contentment? Here in Psalm 84, the birds find places for their nests at the Lord's altars and in his house. They're not homeless. God provides for them. This reminds me of what Jesus taught in his Sermon on the Mount in Matthew 6:25–26:

> Therefore I tell you, do not be anxious about your life, what you will eat or what you will drink, nor about your body, what you will put on. Is not life more than food, and the body more than clothing? Look at the birds of the air: they neither sow

nor reap nor gather into barns, and yet your heavenly Father feeds them. Are you not of more value than they?

Luke described Jesus's teaching about God's kind, generous provision like this: "Consider the ravens: they neither sow nor reap, they have neither storehouse nor barn, and yet God feeds them. Of how much more value are you than the birds!" (Luke 12:24).

The Lord faithfully provides homes and food for the birds. Those birdies don't have to plan ahead, wondering what kind of materials their nests will be made of. Will they find the "right" kind of sticks? Does a strand of yarn or stray bit of fluff fit into their color scheme? Is it what they've been hoping and saving for? Are they working hard with their little bird brains and abilities to get just what they want? Of course not. These feathered friends are content each day. Doesn't it seem like their beautiful songs tell us as much? They don't question their Creator's provision, because he always gives them just what they need.

Jesus went on to use birds as an illustration of important truth in Matthew 10:29: "Are not two sparrows sold for a penny? Yet not one of them will fall to the ground outside your Father's care" (NIV). Dear one, take comfort in this! You can dwell with the Lord and find a home with him, just like the sparrows and swallows and ravens. Birds don't need to sow or reap or gather food into barns, because our heavenly Father feeds them. A bird won't even drop to the ground without our Father's knowledge and care. If he knows and cares for the birds, you can bank on the fact that he knows and cares for you too. He knows your every longing and desire. He knows what you truly need, and he provides in ways you can see—and sometimes in ways you can't.

Turning Head Knowledge into Heart Knowledge

We've seen that contentment with our homes reflects our dependence on and trust in the Lord. But we also know the world is constantly telling us we deserve something different, something better, something more. We can know in our heads that God will provide and that he's provided in the past. We can reason about being content with what we have. But sometimes we need a little extra oomph of encouragement to turn our head knowledge into heart knowledge. So what are a few good, practical ways to encourage contentment?

First of all, I've discovered that my choice of words can make all the difference in the world. When I'm battling discontentment and wishing for something else, changing the language of what I'm saying or thinking has the power to change my attitude and cheer me up. If I see piles of work projects around me in my home (a spot of clutter here, an unfinished renovation there), I can feel overwhelmed by everything that needs my attention, I can get angry with myself or my husband and kids, or I might start to resent having work to do.

But instead of spiraling into thoughts of self-pity, anger, or frustration, I stop and change these internal conversations. One of the easiest ways to start is by exchanging the phrase "I have to" with "I get to." For instance, it's easy to look at the piles of dirty dishes on my kitchen counter and in my sink and think, "I have to wash dishes a third time today!" That phrase stirs up a lot of frustration and angst; it also makes me feel sorry for myself. If I exchange that thought with "I *get* to wash dishes again today!," sure, it sounds a little like Pollyanna or Mary Poppins has taken up residence in my brain, and I may want to cringe at how sugary sweet it all sounds, but it actually helps me think about what a gift it is to have dishes in my home that I love.

Telling myself that I *get* to wash and dry our laundry again reminds me that it's a gift to have so many people in my home I get to dress. It also tells me that the Lord has blessed my family and me with so much clothing and a working washer and dryer. (After needing to use a laundromat for more than a decade, I know these are good gifts.) You can do this with any chore, not just laundry or dishes. With one small word choice, you can adjust your entire attitude and begin to find contentment.

One other trick for cultivating contentment is to look for things you're grateful for. You may want to start a gratitude journal or keep separate notes of all the things, large and small, you appreciate. If you keep these small notes together in a vase, jar, or decorative bowl, you can read through your blessings when you're feeling down. Just like the way you'll remember blessings when you think of what you "get" to do, you'll find so many of them when you're on the lookout for the good things the Lord brings to your day.

Many of our homemaking frustrations might even stem from an abundance of God's provisions. You have too much stuff and decluttering's the reasonable solution? Just think of the way he's entrusted you with so many belongings, and now you get to share your wealth with others! Does it feel like cleaning your home takes a long time? You've been blessed with a lot of space! Is it time to make yet another grocery list and head to the grocery store? You get to choose what you'll eat instead of only getting what someone else doles out!

An attitude of gratitude and thoughtful, positive words have a lot of power when it comes to quieting discontentment. And what's the most powerful antidote of all? Prayer. Simply talk to God. Confess your discontentment to your heavenly Father. Thank him for the good gifts he's given you and thank him for your challenges too. It's okay to admit that you don't know what to do or that you're frustrated and overwhelmed. And then ask him for his help and guidance in creating true contentment in your heart.

Tension Tamer

Remember that your heavenly Father wants to hear from you. He cares. You can cry out to him anytime, anywhere. As you wait for his deliverance:

- **Make an effort to notice the good things he gives or has given you.**

- When you spy his good gifts, write them down.
- At the end of the week, read back over your notes and thank your heavenly Father for the wonderful ways he's blessed you.

Living Happily Ever After

Have you ever noticed that happily-ever-afters typically happen after a climactic struggle? In any good story, plot twists lead the audience astray and suggest that all hope should be lost. The main character seems destined to lose whatever conflict she's enduring. Yet there's always a flicker of hope before joyful resolution. All hope is *not* lost.

Real life stories from history can be like that, too, and we get to see a happy resolution for one such story in Psalm 126. The psalm captures a moment when the Israelites were freed to return to their homes. Some biblical scholars suspect this may have been written after they were released from Babylonian captivity. Psalm 126 describes the great joy they experienced when this deliverance happened:

When the LORD restored the fortunes of Zion,
   we were like those who dream.
Then our mouth was filled with laughter,
   and our tongue with shouts of joy;
then they said among the nations,
   "The LORD has done great things for them."
The LORD has done great things for us;
   we are glad.

> . . . Those who sow in tears
> shall reap with shouts of joy!
> He who goes out weeping,
> bearing the seed for sowing,
> shall come home with shouts of joy,
> bringing his sheaves with him.
>
> (verses 1–3, 5–6)

Getting to return to their home was like a dream come true. And what was the response of the Israelites? Laughter and shouts of joy. This was such an amazing event that even Gentiles could see that only God could make it happen. The Lord did great things for his people.

Have you ever watched this kind of fairy-tale ending work out in your own life or in the life of someone you love?

This psalm vividly reminds me of what happened after my discontentment and depression over my family's downsizing and drastic move to the cramped town house. Knowing that I didn't want to settle into that place, I spent months praying and praying and praying. When my marriage seemed terribly strained and I was certain Aaron and I would be at odds forever, I prayed for a miracle. When I looked outside and felt suffocated by having neighbors so nearby, I prayed for a new house and new neighbors. I prayed I'd have a yard again for our children to enjoy, I prayed the Lord would move my husband to a safe public school district closer to our families, and I prayed for flower gardens. (I truly believe the neighbor garden I described in chapter 3 was a direct answer to these prayers!)

But this chapter of my family's life wasn't solely about a fairy-tale ending. Plenty of good things happened along the way. Through all the togetherness he gave my family in our close quarters, the Lord began to heal my marriage and mend my relationship with my husband. Because we didn't need to spend time maintaining a house, our young family was able to bond with fun activities.

Just when it seemed like we might want to consider a long-term plan in the city where we relocated, the Lord surprised us with a resolution to our situation. When the first year of our lease was almost up, Aaron got a job offer from my alma mater. I was the one to answer the phone call from the principal and hear the good news. When I hung up the phone, I collapsed to my knees and wept, thanking the Lord for his amazing rescue.

When the final moments in our rented townhome came and my husband and I carried load after load of packed boxes from our single-car garage to our moving truck, I wanted to pinch myself to make sure I wasn't dreaming. The Lord provided a way out! Like Aaron had predicted more than a year earlier, we would return from our exile back to our homeland.

After we rolled down the moving truck door and locked the town house, I climbed into the driver's seat of our family's car and squealed with pure joy. My squeal turned into a whoop of thrilled gratitude as I followed Aaron out of the parking lot. The Lord faithfully delivered us. As tears of joy streamed down my face, I prayed out loud, praising God for his rescue. Even if I didn't know what to expect in our family's future, I knew I could trust the Lord.

Like the psalmist described,

> Those who sow in tears
> shall reap with shouts of joy!
> He who goes out weeping,
> bearing the seed for sowing,
> shall come home with shouts of joy,
> bringing his sheaves with him.
> (Psalm 126:5–6)

The day we moved into our town house I wept uncontrollably with sorrow. I experienced sowing in tears. And the day we moved out, I shouted with joy. Through that difficult year, the Lord proved how he could redeem and restore the most unwanted situations. He can provide a wonderful harvest when you least expect it. I've witnessed the way he delivers from the tension of discontentment in my own life, and I'm absolutely sure he can do it in your life as well.

Chapter 13

Fear

Shortly after Aaron and I settled into our first home, my aunt died. The night our family learned of her death, we also uncovered a secret she'd kept hidden for years: She was a hoarder. After authorities opened her front door, they navigated through tall piles of clutter packed into every single room before they reached her body. Instead of asking her family for help, she had kept the burden of her hoarding an awful secret—one that was never resolved in her lifetime.

Once her funeral was over, her brothers and sisters were left with the monumental task of going through her belongings and cleaning up her house to sell. Filled storage units our family didn't even know she'd rented went up for auction. Dollar bills and coins crammed into random containers throughout her home were found, and surprises—like a shopping bag stuffed with half a dozen brand-new clown wigs—filled every room. Hours upon hours of sorting, cleaning, and pitching consumed the family's summer. Several dumpsters were filled with what she had considered to be either treasures or burdens.

While I wasn't a part of the cleanup efforts, walking through the initial mess and hearing the stories of the cleaning process deeply affected me. My aunt might have thought she could hide her messy secrets, but in death everything was made clear. For the next year, I obsessed over cleaning my own home. What if I was a hoarder just waiting to happen? Or what if I suddenly died in a tragic accident? Would my husband know how to find what he needed?

I ruthlessly threw things out, organized and labeled belongings, and brought messy spaces into order. But the truth was, I didn't feel compelled to clean up by my own choice; I was completely scared into doing it. The fear of an untimely death or having people poring over my belongings consumed my thoughts and fueled my actions.

Facing How Fear Changes Us

Our culture has a morbid obsession with fear. If you listen to the news, you know media corporations want you to believe you should worry about a lot of things. In fact, according to the media, we face impending doom every day. Whether you prefer to read your news, skim daily headlines, or get caught up on current events through podcasts, you're likely being continually reminded of the pervasive fright fest.

Not only do fear-inducing headlines result in higher ratings for the media, but they also drive sales of many products, from medicines to insurance to alarm systems to weapons. Because fear sells, retailers and media outlets try to make the most of it. And while sales can be tracked, the way fear adds tension and stress to all aspects of life can't. Fear can change your mindset and your home without you even realizing it. Consider how contemporary events have noticeably shaped our culture:

- September 11 changed the travel industry. If you went to an airport before 2001, anyone could walk inside without security checkpoints or searches, sit down to watch takeoffs and landings inside the airport waiting areas, or go inside to drop off or pick up travelers without any plane tickets.
- The fallout of the Great Recession drastically altered home-buying practices, regulations, and prices.

- COVID-19 affected the mental health and physical practices of people around the world. Before 2020, wearing masks was largely unheard of, and social distancing and quarantining were unimaginable concepts.

Aside from the fear of being involved in a large-scale event, unique fears and concerns woven throughout our own personal stories also shape the way we live. Fear of hoarding, as I experienced, is just one of countless potential fears that can affect how you care for your home.

For example, if you unexpectedly lose your job and are forced to make absolutely every dollar stretch, you might end up selling your belongings as a way to bring in some cash. Instead of being able to move past that experience once you secure a new job and watch your finances rebound, maybe you remain overly cautious and stressed about what you purchase or how much you spend.

If you or a loved one faces a devastating illness, the experience might change the way you manage your home—from the types of cleaning supplies you buy to the frequency or intensity of your housecleaning— even after the crisis is over. You may change your behavior because you're afraid something tragic could happen again.

You may find yourself not wanting to part with your belongings out of fear. The Great Depression changed the way an entire generation of people lived. For the rest of their lives, many people of that generation held on to absolutely everything because what they'd previously owned had been either sold, taken away from them, or utilized until it was useless. The catchphrase for an entire generation was "Use it up, wear it out, make it do, or do without." Decades later, women still reused plastic bread bags over and over because the bags hadn't worn out.

My grandma, who was almost given to an orphanage when her parents ran out of money at the height of the Depression, saved everything as an adult. When I was a girl, I'd help her decorate birthday cakes for family members, and my favorite cakes were "junk cakes." Grandma kept a wooden bowl filled with every plastic prize any of her seven kids had ever pulled out of a cereal or Cracker Jack box. I'd load the cheap, colorful tchotchkes onto a frosted cake, and voilà! It was time for a family celebration.

Just like that wooden bowl of cereal box treasures, Grandma's entire home had collections, unexpected knickknacks, and belongings tucked away in nooks and crannies. Less was not more in her estimation. "Maximalism" brought a sense of security for her.

In the same way that my grandma and other homemakers from the mid-century held on to everything as a way of coping with the uncertainty of the future, you and I have our own quirks too. After living through the supply chain issues of 2020, I now try to buy seasonal goodies as soon as they reach the store, even if it's months in advance. I remember fretting over Easter baskets after being stuck at home and sick during the pandemic. My in-store shopper did a great job finding what she could at the store that Easter, but I don't want to feel that unprepared again. So now, when boxes of Valentine chocolates pop up on store shelves as soon as Christmas is over, I buy a couple and keep them tucked away until February. When Thanksgiving turkey sales begin sometime in October, I buy one frozen bird just in case they won't be available later.

Aware of the hoarding tendencies in my family, I try not to buy too much. But I also want to be prepared and plan ahead. I think more along the lines of Proverbs 6:6–8 instead of flying by the seat of my pants:

> Go to the ant, O sluggard;
>> consider her ways, and be wise.
> Without having any chief,
>> officer, or ruler,

she prepares her bread in summer
and gathers her food in harvest.

My planner tendencies have ramped up due to my trying to prepare for the unexpected.

Refusing to Live in Fear

Throughout the Bible, we read that believers in the living God don't have to exist in fear. As Paul wrote to Timothy, "God has not given us a spirit of timidity, but of power and love and discipline" (2 Timothy 1:7 NASB).

We love, honor, and serve the God of angel armies. He is the all-powerful Lord Almighty. Psalm 66:1–7 (NIV) reminds us:

Shout for joy to God, all the earth!
Sing the glory of his name;
make his praise glorious.
Say to God, "How awesome are your deeds!
So great is your power
that your enemies cringe before you.
All the earth bows down to you;
they sing praise to you,
they sing the praises of your name."

Come and see what God has done,
his awesome deeds for mankind!
He turned the sea into dry land,
they passed through the waters on foot—
come, let us rejoice in him.
He rules forever by his power.

His deeds are awesome, and his power is amazing. He has done astounding things for humankind in the past and will continue to do so. God protects and provides for his children. He guides and gives them all they require. He delivers and delights in them. I will say it again, because we need to soak this truth in: *We don't have to live in fear.*

Psalm 78:52–53 (NIV) recalls the Lord's faithful protection and provision for his people:

> He brought his people out like a flock;
>> he led them like sheep through the wilderness.
> He guided them safely, so they were unafraid.

Just as he took care of the Israelites, he will always take care of his children. If you trust and worship him, he will bring you out of life's snares and lead you through your wilderness. He will guide you safely, and you can be unafraid.

Examples for living a bold, unafraid life of trust are woven throughout the psalms. David, a man who was familiar with running for his very life, wrote about the faithful protection of the Lord over and over. For example, in Psalm 145:13–20 (NIV), David sang praises for all the Lord does:

> The LORD is trustworthy in all he promises
>> and faithful in all he does.
> The LORD upholds all who fall
>> and lifts up all who are bowed down.
> The eyes of all look to you,
>> and you give them their food at the proper time.
> You open your hand
>> and satisfy the desires of every living thing.
>
> The LORD is righteous in all his ways
>> and faithful in all he does.

The LORD is near to all who call on him,
    to all who call on him in truth.
He fulfills the desires of those who fear him;
    he hears their cry and saves them.
The LORD watches over all who love him,
    but all the wicked he will destroy.

Through these praises, we observe our God's awesome character and attributes: He's faithful in all his words; he's kind in all his works; he is righteous not just sometimes when he feels like it, but in all his ways.

We also see the amazing things he does: He upholds those who fall, he raises up those who are bowed down, he gives food and satisfies the desire of every living thing, he is near to all who call on him in truth, he fulfills the desires of and hears and saves those who fear him, and he preserves all who love him. When we slow down to ponder him, how can we possibly let fear grip us? What do we have to fear if the Lord is on our side?

Tension Tamer

God's faithful protection is described throughout Psalm 145. If you're wrestling with how much you'd prefer to trust him, remember to do these things:

- Call on him in truth, especially when you're feeling far off but want to be near to him.
- Live with a healthy fear and respect of him, even when you start to doubt that he will listen to or fulfill your desires.
- Love him, even when you long for him to preserve you.

Climbing Out on a Limb of Faith

Whether you've just started following the Lord or have walked with him for years, chances are you've experienced his faithful provision. Throughout my life, I've gone out on plenty of limbs with the Lord, trusting him to provide and guide when I step out in faith. Never, ever has he left me in a lurch. Never, ever has he not come through. He has been faithful, time and time again. Even when I've questioned his ways, he has gently guided my path.

Fresh out of college, I followed God's leading to a job on the staff of a missions magazine based in the middle of Virginia. It was the first time I relocated out of state and moved where I didn't know a single soul, eight hours from my family's home. In a pre-internet world, trying to find an apartment in my price range when I lived out of state was a big challenge. Intending to find a place to live on a two-day visit, I searched and searched yet realized that nothing was working out. I didn't know what to do. How could I move somewhere to start a new job if I didn't have a place to live?

Discouraged after the full day of apartment hunting, I returned to a bargain of a motel room with my mom and her best friend to scour apartment ads in the newspaper. Staring off into space toward the room's severely matted, bright scarlet shag carpet, my faith began to waver. I had been so certain that this job and move was the Lord's will for me. But what if I had misunderstood his leading? If I couldn't find a place to live, should I even take the job?

That night, in my desperation, I turned to Psalm 37. Praying it out loud, I noticed how phrases of the psalm brimmed with hope for the hopeless. Thousands of years after the psalm had been written, those instructions fit my life on that disheartening night in Virginia. They continued to fit my life on countless other nights when it seemed like problems and challenges were stacking up against me. And the commands still fit my life and yours right now.

So what are some of the hope-filled, timeless truths David shared? What can encourage us to walk faithfully with the Lord when we face moments of fear?

> Commit your way to the LORD;
>   trust in him, and he will act.
> He will bring forth your righteousness as the light,
>   and your justice as the noonday.
>
> Be still before the LORD and wait patiently for him.
>   (verses 5–7)

> The LORD knows the days of the blameless,
>   and their heritage will remain forever;
> they are not put to shame in evil times;
>   in the days of famine they have abundance.
>   (verses 18–19)

> The steps of a man are established by the LORD,
>   when he delights in his way;
> though he fall, he shall not be cast headlong,
>   for the LORD upholds his hand.

> I have been young, and now am old,
>   yet I have not seen the righteous forsaken
>   or his children begging for bread.
> He is ever lending generously,
>   and his children become a blessing.
>   (verses 23–26)

> Mark the blameless and behold the upright,
>   for there is a future for the man of peace. . . .

The salvation of the righteous is from the LORD;
    he is their stronghold in the time of trouble.
The LORD helps them and delivers them;
    he delivers them from the wicked and saves
        them,
    because they take refuge in him.

(verses 37, 39–40)

Notice all the hope and promise in David's words? He talked about the Lord's action and provision, his protection and deliverance. David used words like *abundance, establish,* and *uphold,* as well as *generous, blessing,* and *future.* Fear disappears when we slow down to meditate on these biblical truths.

Throughout Psalm 37, David guided us by spelling out some specific things to do. We're instructed to "trust in the LORD" (verse 3); "dwell in the land and befriend faithfulness" (verse 3); "delight yourself in the LORD" (verse 4); "commit your way to the LORD," knowing that when you do trust in God, "he will act" (verse 5); "be still before the LORD" (verse 7); keep the Lord's way (verse 34); and wait patiently for him (verses 7, 9, 34). In other words, settle down in safety, abide, and rest in peace. For the Israelites, the ability to live in the land was a powerful blessing; it was their promised land! Living there, in the land of milk and honey, was a gift.

These imperative instructions directly helped the Israelites of David's day, yet they are as timely for us right now as they were back then. We receive so many blessings when we use self-control to let go of fear and choose what's right. And what *is* always right? Keeping the Lord's way, committing our ways to him, delighting ourselves in him, and trusting him.

As we live out these commands in our daily lives, not only will we live a righteous life that pleases the Lord, but our fears will also melt away.

Tension Tamer

David's top three instructions in Psalm 37, restated again and again, are essential for a fearless life:

- Do good.
- Don't fret.
- Wait for the Lord.

What would your life look like if you were committed to doing good? Choosing not to fret? Waiting for the Lord instead of taking matters into your own hands?

Hearing Versus Doing

David could write Psalm 37 about this fearless approach to life because he lived it out in both easy and hard times. And I can easily repeat his instructions and say that we should do them. But hearing what to do and living it out are two different things, aren't they?

So often, it seems like there's a great divide between what we know we need to do and our actual follow through. For example, I know what I need to eat to feel good and have a healthy life. I know how many glasses of water I should drink a day and how much exercise I need to add to each week. But unless I actually eat nutritious foods, drink enough water, and do the exercises, knowing details about a healthy lifestyle doesn't help me. I have to know what to do and then do it. I have to turn all the head knowledge into heart knowledge and obedience. It's as simple and as complicated as the wise advice given in James 1:22: "Don't just listen to God's word. You must do what it says. Otherwise, you are only fooling yourselves" (NLT).

So how do we move beyond fooling ourselves? How do we choose to live a good life that's free from fretting and actually follow through? How do we wait for the Lord without fear of the future?

In moments when I struggle with these choices, especially when worry enters the picture without my invitation, I've found that spiritual breathing helps a lot. A principle I learned from Cru as a college student, spiritual breathing involves exhaling and confessing our sins and doubts and fears. All the things that make me feel like I'm being strangled by worry and doubt? I confess them in a big exhale. I get them out of my heart and mind.

Exhaling and releasing everything to the Lord in surrender is the first step, and inhaling comes next. As I inhale, I ask the Lord to lead and guide me. I breathe out the fear that holds me captive, and I breathe in the freedom, fresh air, and new life that comes from surrendering to Christ.

I wish my aunt who struggled with hoarding would have experienced this fresh air of freedom in Christ. I wish my grandma could have exhaled the bondage of a lifelong attachment to belongings. And if you're struggling with the tension that comes from fear of the known or unknown in your home, I hope and pray you'll practice spiritual breathing to work toward experiencing freedom for yourself.

Tension Tamer

Pause for a moment and try spiritual breathing:

- First, exhale and confess your sins and doubts to the Lord. Release everything to him. Get it all out.
- Next, inhale the freedom of surrender to Christ, knowing he can and will lead you.
- Enjoy the refreshment and peace that he alone can give.

Surrendering Your Fears

My desperate night in the outdated Virginia motel was redeemed by
the Lord guiding me through spiritual breathing in Psalm 37. As I sat
in bed, reading Psalm 37 out loud as a prayer, I exhaled my fears. The
doubts and questions I experienced were laid at his feet in a breath of
surrender. I came to the end of myself and the end of my understanding. Truly, in my heart of hearts, I didn't care what happened next. If
the Lord wanted me to move and serve him in that new job, he would
provide a home. And if he wanted something else, I'd walk away.

The next morning, I called a local church, and the secretary told me
about a couple who wanted a renter for their family's basement apartment. In the matter of a few hours, I ended up walking through a clean
apartment in a Christian home that fit my price range, signing a lease,
and starting my drive back to Ohio, thinking of how I could move in
and decorate my first apartment.

For most Christians I know, and as I've found to be true in my own
life, the Lord often works most powerfully when we come to the end of
ourselves and at what often feels like the last minute. Like the Israelites
facing the Red Sea in Exodus 14, terror can arise when you know you
can't remedy a situation on your own. Psalm 136 recounts the Israelites' exodus and ways the Lord provided:

> To him who divided the Red Sea in two . . .
> and made Israel pass through the midst of it . . .
> but overthrew Pharaoh and his host in the Red Sea,
>   for his steadfast love endures forever.
>   (verses 13–15)

Whether I've faced loss, seemingly impossible deadlines, or situations that looked like unscalable mountains, every single time I have
watched the Lord come through in miraculous ways. His steadfast love
truly endures forever. Because of this, I know I don't have to be held

captive under the tension of fear in my life or in my home. You don't have to either. We can move away from lives of fear into lives of faith, fully knowing that although God's ways may be completely unlike anything we'd ever guess, they will always be good. We don't have to manage our homes in fear of the future. We can live with freedom. The key to unshackling ourselves from our fears is surrendering them first to God, and then waiting for him.

He always, always, always follows through. And when we trust him completely, he'll relieve us from the tension of fear.

Chapter 14

You

IT HAPPENED YET again. After reading a homemaking blog, I felt ashamed for not keeping a predictable daily routine. As hard as I tried, I just couldn't get myself out of bed at the crack of dawn to squeeze in exercise and time with the Lord before my early-rising son raced downstairs. Maybe this had everything to do with the fact that I stayed up later than I should most weeknights for my online side hustle. Or maybe I just wasn't disciplined enough.

As a mom of two toddlers, my days went by in a blur. Between potty training and trying to make healthy, homemade, "real" food, I spent my waking hours trying to do what was best for my young family. We read books and made crafts and spent time playing outside in our yard and at local playgrounds. We made lemonade for our elderly neighbors in the summer and got involved with our church on Sunday mornings and Wednesday nights. An old-fashioned, idyllic childhood was exactly what I hoped to give my son and daughter. And when they were napping or tucked into bed at night, I tried to earn a little extra money from home.

But in the middle of trying so hard to do the right things for my children, I was continually reminded of my struggle to stick to a daily schedule. Shouldn't I make sure I was doing certain chores at certain times?

Was I slacking as a mom because I didn't have my sleepyhead daughter out of bed and at the breakfast table by eight o'clock every morning?

For me, even though the rigidity of a daily routine didn't motivate me, the thought of *not* keeping to a strict schedule made me feel like a mediocre mother. Surely I was failing in my roles as a wife, mom, and homemaker if I didn't go grocery shopping on the same day of the week or know the specific time I'd clean our toilet. While those examples sound laughable, the pressure of judging myself against an unwritten standard of routines brought an unwanted and unnecessary burden. My constant efforts yet forgetfulness to follow through on regular routines left me feeling guilty and upset that I was naturally a night owl instead of a morning person.

Because I genuinely wanted more effective ways to care for my home and kids, I searched for ideas online. But instead of finding encouragement or solutions, I experienced shame and guilt. Blogs left me feeling like a slacker. Images reminded me of how imperfect my home was in comparison. Social media posts showed everyone else's spotless homes while I struggled with the frustration of picking up after my children. It made me wonder, even if I could figure out a *plan* to do more, how would I ever find enough *energy* to do everything? What was I doing wrong?

Tension Tamer

Maybe sticking to a predictable rhythm in your day is where you shine the brightest. Or perhaps you feel like you're at your best when you're going with the flow and managing the daily challenges of life as they come. But stop and think for a moment about something: Do you feel better about yourself when you follow a routine and worse when you don't? If so, why do you think that is?

I wish someone would've told me that everything was okay. I was giving my children, husband, and home my best, and that was enough. In fact, my best was probably more than enough. Did it truly matter if I couldn't wake up at 5:00 a.m. to get a head start on my day? No way. A good night of sleep was the best choice for my exhausted body and mind. Was it a realistic expectation to have a perpetually tidy home in the middle of raising two little people? Not by a long shot.

If wiser women did try to communicate that message of grace to me, their voices were drowned out by the distraction of immaculate home renovations on television, commercials about picture-perfect holiday entertaining, and flawless photos from mommy bloggers.

When we feel weighed down by our homes—whether we're stressed about tending to daily chores, we feel like we must decorate in a certain way, or we're completely overwhelmed by a never-ending, ever-increasing to-do list—we can usually identify plenty of outside factors that contribute to our tension, as I've mentioned in previous chapters. We might struggle because we've bought into advertising or given in to peer pressure. Dealing with spoken and unspoken expectations from family members may be an issue that nags us incessantly. Handling all the chaos and demands on our time may affect the way we care for our home. We might also notice specific internal factors adding to our stress. Adoring (or even worshipping) our belongings, holding on to too much stuff, dwelling in discontentment, and facing fears can all be very real challenges to our desire to create and enjoy peaceful homes. And sometimes the biggest culprit causing tension in our homes is ourselves.

Juggling All. The. Things.

Far too often we think we need to get everything together and keep everything together without giving ourselves any grace. Instead of realizing weaknesses or circumstances might be in our way, we think we need to possess superpowers that are not only impossible but also impractical. When we don't measure up to some fantastical ideal, we get disappointed and try to do more.

In many ways, we're trying to be Superwoman by juggling all. the. things. If we could find a way to keep up with our house and take care of our kids and manage groceries and keep schedules and spend some kind of quality time with our husbands all while tackling a side hustle, we'd have basically transformed ourselves into Superwoman. Getting all that work done every single day—or let's keep things real, *any* day!—would be nothing short of leaping tall buildings in single bounds. There are days when that level of earthly perfection seems within our power to attain, until we make one small misstep and our carefully juggled balls come crashing to the ground.

Ready for a reality check? Superwoman is a fictional character. If you'd prefer Wonder Woman and her Invisible Plane, she's fictional too. They're both completely made up. When we attempt to be Superwoman, it's as silly as trying to emulate any other cartoon character, from SpongeBob SquarePants to Bugs Bunny.

If you feel like you need a fantastic role model, though, let me tell you about a real woman who cared for her home and family in an amazing way. The woman described in the thirty-first chapter of Proverbs was both real and super in what she did.

Meeting a Really Super Woman

At the end of the Old Testament book of Proverbs is a thorough description of a woman written by a King Lemuel, which may or may not have been a pen name for the real author. Some scholars suspect the author was King Solomon, who wrote not only much of the advice in Proverbs but also several psalms. If Solomon did write this portion of Proverbs, he may have been writing what he learned from his mother, Bathsheba, since Scripture begins this proverb with "an oracle that his mother taught him." Whoever King Lemuel was, he passed along some great advice for what men should wisely look for in a woman.

As the Proverbs 31 woman lived and worked diligently thousands of years ago, she used wisdom to manage much in her home, family, and career. While Proverbs 31 gives specific details, some of the basic highlights are that this woman ran her own business, made savvy decisions, provided for her family, and managed her household well. Not only was this woman trustworthy, but she also wasn't afraid to share her wisdom and kindness with others. That's a lot to handle today, let alone thousands of years before Jesus's birth, when women were viewed and treated very differently.

Even with her exceptionally good work ethic and admirable character traits, she didn't attempt all the work by herself. Other people helped her. (You can read Proverbs 31:10–31 for details.) And she didn't have to do everything in her own power because, like David expresses in Psalm 73:26, even if her flesh and her heart failed, God was the strength of her heart and her portion forever. This woman didn't just have noble character; she was also praiseworthy because of her fear of the Lord.

Maybe the most encouraging realization is that this woman didn't exhaust herself by doing absolutely all. the. things. every single day of her life. Rather, Proverbs 31 gives us a fantastic picture of the *culmination* of a woman's life. It's highlighting her greatest hits. Encompassing all the responsibilities throughout the seasons of her life, the description shows us the total amount of good she accomplished in her lifetime.

Please keep this lifelong perspective in mind. Just like the Proverbs 31 woman didn't attempt to do every single feat listed in this proverb every single day or even every single year, you and I don't have to exhaust ourselves by attempting the impossible. Often tensions come through our own expectations, which may not be reasonable. So many times, we expect ourselves to do absolutely everything with complete excellence every single day, and when we have a string of days as normal humans, we get disappointed and frustrated. But like you show your BFF a lot of grace when she's juggling many roles and responsibilities, it's time you start showing yourself a whole lot of grace too.

Accepting Our Imperfections

Despite the work and stress our homes may add to our lives, there's a reason there's no place like home. Because our homes have the potential to be places of rest and refreshment for ourselves and many others, they're worth our effort!

Instead of giving myself the benefit of the doubt or showing some compassionate understanding, I'm the first to judge myself when I can't meet my own unrealistically high expectations. I do this in my everyday life, and I do this when it comes to caring for my home. I'm harder on myself than I am on any other person on the planet.

For example, when I'm strapped for time, I know I can't tackle the monumental tasks in my home and make much headway. Yet instead of owning up to the fact that I'm trying to juggle too much and that perfection is something I need to let go of, I get angry with myself for being such a mess maker or not being more organized. If only I filed away necessary paperwork alphabetically instead of gathering it together in one big pile, maybe I wouldn't feel so frazzled. Instead of remembering that I've struggled with this same tendency my entire adult life or recognizing that my commitments aren't slowing down, my high expectations immediately swing to self-judgment.

Here's the thing, though: We're not perfect. And in this lifetime, we will never be perfect. We live in a fallen world; things in our homes will naturally break, wear out, and get messy. That is reality. Why we hold ourselves to impractical, impossible standards is something I can't fully understand.

Despite the fact that perfection is out of reach, we can continue to make efforts to care for our homes. Most days, making time for some sort of work around the house helps maintain a home that's good enough. It's completely okay to work toward the "perfect" mark. But we can't forget that actual perfection is unachievable and that we can't judge ourselves against impossible standards.

For me and many others, our homes never seem like they're clean enough. One of my blog readers, Katrina, opened up about her expectations for her own life, home, and family:

> For me, the pressure I feel is certainly internal. My family can sit amongst the clutter and be content, but for me, the pressure to juggle a nine-to-five job outside of the home, then come home and create the time and space to cook, clean, be a wife, be a mom—some days it's a lot and I crave time to just sit and *be* and enjoy my home the way my family does.

Another blog reader, Stacey, shared a similar sentiment:

> The biggest stress on me is the stress I put on myself. There is so much I want to be able to do for my family. I want to cook meals from scratch, have a garden with an abundant supply of fruits and veggies, keep a clean house, do things with my kids, crochet more for extra money. The truth is I'm enjoying this so much that the days are passing quickly and I can't allot enough time to accomplish each thing daily. I could take a whole day, sometimes two days, for each thing and still not be satisfied with the progress. I still find more to be done.

I echo Katrina's and Stacey's ambitions and struggles. I get it. I've often imagined living in a world with forty-hour days, six-week months, or fourteen-month years, just so I might have a better chance to finish what I'd like around the house. It's tempting to want to do all. the. things. all. the. time. And with excellence. While I don't think wanting to do so much is necessarily problematic, trouble brews when we get upset with ourselves for not actually accomplishing everything we hoped to do.

Many days, my husband asks me what my plans are. I start off sharing one or two of my top priorities, then pause before launching into a list of about twenty more things I hope to do. Clearly, believing I can do so much in one day is ridiculous. And if I truly think I have to accomplish every dream task every day, I'm setting myself up for disappointment. It doesn't hurt to dream, but you and I simply must stop judging ourselves based on how much we get done or how well we're running our house on any given day. We have to stop holding ourselves hostage to our to-do lists.

Giving Yourself Grace

Think about someone you know and love dearly. When this person makes an innocent mistake, do you think less of her? Do you tear this person down with your thoughts and words? Do you berate her and doubt she'll ever be able to improve? Do you hold a grudge?

I'm going to go out on a limb and guess that you wouldn't think of treating someone you love in this way! I suspect you would see past her mistake with grace and forgiveness and then hope for the best. You might even try to see how you can help her out.

If we are so willing to look at *others* with grace and understanding, why in the world are we so quick to hold *ourselves* to impossibly high standards?

If I walked through your door right now and peeked at the problem spots in your home, I wouldn't dream of wagging my finger at you or shaking my head in judgment. Instead, I'd remind you of everything you're trying to juggle. I'd try to help you figure out what's at the root of your weaknesses and brainstorm potential solutions. I'd congratulate you and help you celebrate what you're doing well. And I'd encourage you to keep doing a great job. I hope you'd do the same for me if you came to my house!

Of course, we aren't going to show up on each other's doorsteps. But what if we could be that kind of friend to ourselves? What if we could give ourselves a little more grace?

This idea of not being so harsh on yourself and giving yourself grace is nothing new. Hebrews 4:14–16 gives us a good picture of someone who understands our struggles and is ready and willing to show us grace:

> Since we have a great high priest who has ascended into heaven, Jesus the Son of God, let us hold firmly to the faith we profess. For we do not have a high priest who is unable to empathize with our weaknesses, but we have one who has been tempted in every way, just as we are—yet he did not sin. Let us then approach God's throne of grace with confidence, so that we may receive mercy and find grace to help us in our time of need. (NIV)

Jesus can and does empathize with our weaknesses. Because of Jesus, we can confidently approach God and receive mercy and grace. How is this possible? The apostle Paul explained God's grace, a gift we couldn't ever earn or deserve, and detailed this incredible offer for all. In Romans 3:22–24, he wrote:

> We are made right with God by placing our faith in Jesus Christ. And this is true for everyone who believes, no matter who we are.
>
>   For everyone has sinned; we all fall short of God's glorious standard. Yet God, in his grace, freely makes us right in his sight. He did this through Christ Jesus when he freed us from the penalty for our sins. (NLT)

Just as our homes fall short of our own standards, we *all* fall short of God's standard. Absolutely none of us is perfect. No, not one. But we don't have to live in that defeat. Through Christ, and Christ alone, we're made right in God's sight. Romans 5:1–2 spells this out:

> Since we have been made right in God's sight by faith, we have peace with God because of what Jesus Christ our Lord has done for us. Because of our faith, Christ has brought us into this place of undeserved privilege where we now stand, and we confidently and joyfully look forward to sharing God's glory. (NLT)

By God's grace, we're made right in his sight—we don't face condemnation from him. As Romans 8:1 teaches us, "There is therefore now no condemnation for those who are in Christ Jesus." Instead, we receive undeserved privilege and peace with God. If you've welcomed Jesus into your life through faith, he doesn't condemn you. Why condemn yourself?

God is calling to us, whether we recognize his voice or not. And he invites us to fulfill the persistent longing in our hearts and dwell in a forever home with him. Think about getting to dwell with the Lord—inhabiting a home with the Lord of the universe. Isn't it amazing that he will abide with us? That we can remain with him for all eternity?

This is absolutely true. So why do we still search for our worth or validation of ourselves in our homes?

In a world that's filled with distractions, it's easy to silence the distinct call of the Lord. Entertainment, food, drink, clothing, travel, and our very homes and possessions can absorb our attention and hijack our hearts. We focus on and worship idols we've constructed. And if following our fancies isn't enough of a distraction, it's easy for God's still, small voice to get drowned out with the nonstop noise of our current age.

Feeling Sheepish

Because of our propensity for being distracted, people are often compared to sheep in the Bible. Just like sheep, we have a tendency to wander off. As Peter wrote in a letter to the early church, "You were straying like sheep, but have now returned to the Shepherd and Overseer of your souls" (1 Peter 2:25).

Intelligent and resistant to change, sheep are social animals who love to bond closely with their flock, and often they flee together as a defense mechanism of sorts. Capable of solving problems, sheep respond to food, have a great memory, recognize their own names, and are able to distinguish their shepherd's face and voice from those of strangers.[1]

With his firsthand knowledge of the traits of sheep, David, a former shepherd, began Psalm 23 with the words, "The Lord is my shepherd, I lack nothing" (niv). Throughout the rest of this well-known psalm, David explained how our Shepherd provides for and protects us, his own flock of sheep:

> He makes me lie down in green pastures,
>   he leads me beside quiet waters,
>   he refreshes my soul.
> He guides me along the right paths
>   for his name's sake.
> Even though I walk
>   through the darkest valley,
> I will fear no evil,
>   for you are with me.
>
>   (verses 2–4 niv)

After outlining this beautiful picture of the Lord leading and caring for us as our good Shepherd, David concluded with an interesting turn:

> You prepare a table before me
>   in the presence of my enemies.

You anoint my head with oil;
my cup overflows.
Surely your goodness and love will follow me
all the days of my life,
and I will dwell in the house of the LORD
forever.

(verses 5–6 NIV)

After David's talk of being shepherded along a journey, suddenly we're presented with a table.

What is the significance of this table? And why would the Lord, our Shepherd, choose to prepare a table for us right there in front of everyone? Even in front of our enemies? Frankly, if I were planning to host a dinner, I'd choose to only include my friends or family. Yet it's vital to remember that fractured relationships don't stop our Lord. You don't have to get along perfectly with everyone in order for Jesus to care for you, guide, or honor you. He cares for you even when you have strained relationships with others.

If he's preparing a table for you right now (and he is), it's on display for everyone to see. Friend and foe, believer and unbeliever alike.

No matter what tension you're facing the most right now—whether you feel overwhelmed with the state of your home, face strained relationships, or have lost your own peace of mind—God's still inviting you to live with him. If you are a believer in Christ—you've trusted him as your Savior and Shepherd, your Guide and your God—his goodness and mercy will follow you today and every day for the rest of your life. Whatever tensions you feel, he's still getting his table ready for you.

Dwelling Forever

Once you're rescued by God's grace through faith in Jesus, there's more than freedom from condemnation. There's more than mercy and grace. You get to experience a relationship with the Lord of the universe. You don't have to worry about feeling these tensions of tidy for eternity, because there is no tension in an eternity spent with Jesus. You can anticipate tension-free immortality. You get to look forward to dwelling with God in the heavenly home that he's preparing for you even now. As Jesus taught in John 14:1–4:

> Do not let your hearts be troubled. You believe in God; believe also in me. My Father's house has many rooms; if that were not so, would I have told you that I am going there to prepare a place for you? And if I go and prepare a place for you, I will come back and take you to be with me that you also may be where I am. You know the way to the place where I am going. (NIV)

The way to that place is through Jesus. *He* is the way. (Two verses later, in John 14:6, he shared that he's not only the way but also the truth and the life.) If you believe in him, you don't have to let your heart be troubled. You don't have to be troubled by the pressure of perfection that the world creates. You don't have to be troubled by your own personal pressure for perfection. You don't have to be troubled when well-intentioned people add to your stress. And you don't have to be troubled when circumstances like work, the busyness and chaos of life, clutter, discontentment, or fear threaten to drag you down.

When the Lord is your dwelling place, you can feast on his goodness and mercy. You can sit back and relax at his table of abundance that he's prepared just for you. You are invited and you are welcome.

David described the table and a cup in Psalm 23:5 (NIV):

> You prepare a table before me
>   in the presence of my enemies.
> You anoint my head with oil;
>   my cup overflows.

What does this mean for you and me? Max Lucado explains the significance of the cup:

> The overflowing cup was a powerful symbol in the days of David. Hosts in the ancient East used it to send a message to the guest. As long as the cup was kept full, the guest knew he was welcome. But when the cup sat empty, the host was hinting that the hour was late. On those occasions, however, when the host especially enjoyed the company of the person, he filled the cup to overflowing. He didn't stop when the wine reached the rim; he kept pouring until the liquid ran over the edge of the cup and down on the table.[2]

As frequent hosts of dinner parties, my family can remember dinners where we'd let the glasses empty quickly, and other dinners where we'd go out of our way to continue filling cups to overflowing. On those special evenings, we didn't want to say goodbye for the night. We wished our guests could stay with our family forever. The amazing reality is that our Lord loves his chosen ones so much, he has prepared a table for us and wants us to stay. We can linger around his table; we don't have to leave. We get to dwell with him forever.

David lived on the run without a home of his own, but later took up residence in a palace as a king! He knew, regardless of where he might live, that he could spend his life on earth with the Lord:

> One thing I ask from the LORD,
>   this only do I seek:
> that I may dwell in the house of the LORD
>   all the days of my life,
> to gaze on the beauty of the LORD
>   and to seek him in his temple.
> For in the day of trouble

> he will keep me safe in his dwelling;
> he will hide me in the shelter of his sacred tent
> and set me high upon a rock.
>
> (Psalm 27:4–5 NIV)

Clearly, David knew he could experience a dwelling with the Lord in the present moment and all the days of his life. But he also recognized that he had an eternal future with his heavenly Father, as he wrote in Psalm 61:1–5 (NIV):

> Hear my cry, O God;
> listen to my prayer.
>
> From the ends of the earth I call to you,
> I call as my heart grows faint;
> lead me to the rock that is higher than I.
> For you have been my refuge,
> a strong tower against the foe.
>
> I long to dwell in your tent forever
> and take refuge in the shelter of your wings.
> For you, God, have heard my vows;
> you have given me the heritage of those who fear your name.

As long as we're here on earth, we can and should emulate David and long to dwell in the Lord's tent forever and be face-to-face with him. When we experience that homesickness, we can take refuge in the shelter of the Lord's wings. He's our refuge and shelter no matter where we live or what our earthly homes look like. While we wait for our heavenly dwelling, he protects us completely as we remain close to him here on earth.

Craving Order

While we're living this life, the tension of tidy is real. God created this earth with order, and he holds all things together. Colossians 1:16–17 tells us about Christ's role in this: "In him all things were created: things in heaven and on earth, visible and invisible, whether thrones or powers or rulers or authorities; all things have been created through him and for him. He is before all things, and in him all things hold together" (NIV). Because our Creator is a God of order, it's natural that we—his creation—crave order too. After all, we're made in his image.

Craving order is one thing. But feeling strangled by the weight and pressure of perfection through tidiness is something else. Unfortunately, we are the ones who magnify the strain and stress in our homes.

Deep down, at the core of our tension, it's you and me.

Our own cleanliness preferences, the unique ways we each deal with our messes, and our individual challenges and pressures only build the tension. If we feel like it's a crushing load, it's because it is. But the reality of our messes isn't going to change. Messes are as certain as the scientific law of entropy.

Just in case you need a science refresher, entropy is the process by which everything declines to disorder. When a house or yard is left alone without any upkeep, you'll see entropy in action.

Over the course of our marriage, Aaron and I have bought three different houses, and throughout our three house hunts, we've walked through more than two hundred unique properties. (What can I say? We're both particular and each have specific preferences.) Some houses were immaculate and gorgeous, but other houses should have been condemned. Every home had been in new and excellent condition at one time, but neglect had taken its toll in frightening ways:

- We walked through century-old homes that needed not only thorough cleaning but also new heating and cooling units, windows, roofs, electricity, kitchens, and bathrooms. The only aspects that didn't appear to require massive work were the basic frames of the houses, but based on the condition of the rest of the houses, I doubt we looked closely enough.

- In one house, we walked down the basement steps to find four feet of standing water everywhere.
- Two other houses had huge cracks along the entire length of their basement foundation walls.
- A few houses had dead leaves blowing in the rooms because of the broken and missing windows.
- Before we toured one house where gargoyles decorated the basement, we had to sign a waiver that we wouldn't press legal charges if we were harmed on the property.

I can assure you, entropy is very real in homes! On a smaller scale, in our everyday lives, entropy simply means once we clean our houses, they will get dirty again. We might appreciate and seek order in our lives, but it will never be perfect or permanent on this side of heaven. Once we accept that and stop beating ourselves up over the inevitable—that perfection is impossible—we can start to break free from the tension.

Living It Out

By now, you and I both know that we *should* let the Lord reign over our hearts and homes. We *should* surrender and let him do his good work. But then, when we look around and see piles of laundry in hampers and dusty cobwebs stretching in corners or feel our bare feet sticking to the kitchen floor, it can be way too easy to turn right back into our flipped-out, overwhelmed, speed-cleaning selves who just want to get. things. picked. up before we lose our self-control and start venting!

When you find yourself falling headfirst into unrealistic expectations for yourself or feel like you might crumble under the weight of your own pressure and demands, stop. Literally choose to stop your thoughts. Take a deep breath, and remember your good Shepherd. Before you do another thing in your home, take a moment to invest in your relationship with him, whether it's through prayer, reading the Psalms, or singing praise to him. This will seem counterproductive to getting done what you wanted to get done, but the point is not productivity. You desperately need to take your eyes off yourself, your circumstances, and your stuff. Forget about your home and your ideals. Just stop to connect with the Lord of the universe. When you recognize, honor, and worship *him*, you get your eyes off yourself and break free from the tension.

If you wake up tomorrow and all the overwhelm comes rushing back into your mind, stop yourself again. And again. And again. Anytime the tensions try to steal your peace, stop to remember the Lord. He's always there, offering you loving rest and freedom, if only you'll take it.

The mess that is your house might be the cherry on top of the overwhelming, tension-filled sundae of your life. You might feel completely buried under the weight of everyone who wants more of you, including your kids, who want more of your time; your husband, who would love to ask you for more attention if you weren't so busy and grouchy about your unfinished to-do list; and your parents, who wish you visited more often and stayed longer. You might be far behind with tasks at work and outside the home. Your help might be desperately needed at church and a hundred different organizations that are all doing good things. It's like your life and time and attention are hemorrhages that won't stop gushing.

But God doesn't ask you to do more. *He* is the one who must increase, not you, as John 3:30 tells us. You already know you're weary. No one has to tell you that you're heavy-laden. So God invites you to come to him and offers you the gift of rest (Matthew 11:28). Even in messy moments of life, when absolutely nothing seems remotely close to being orderly, you can be still and know that he is God. He is the one who will free you from all the tension in your life, your home, and your heart.

With the grace of God, it's possible to close the door on your messiest room, walk away, and know that it's okay to move on with the rest of your day. (Because, truly, it is.)

We don't have to carry the crippling weight of tension alone. When we're in the middle of our struggles, we can remember the truth from Psalm 68:19: "Blessed be the Lord, who daily bears our burden, the God who is our salvation" (NASB). *He* is the one who bears our burden every single day. We don't have to attempt to bear our own. We already know it's heavier than we can bear.

If we'll take our eyes off the chores and messes and stresses in our homes, if we'll truly rest in our burden-bearing Lord and keep our minds on him, he'll keep us in perfect peace (see Isaiah 26:3). It's possible to stop laboring and straining with that never-ending to-do list. And it's possible to keep our eyes and hearts focused on our Savior instead.

When we do, we can watch him move into our homes and use them for his will and his good work. We can work hard for God's glory, but he'll be the one to multiply our efforts and do the good work of building our homes. As we decrease in our own tired attempts to bring our homes under our control, he will increase. He is the one who can and will bring freedom. As we focus on him and him alone, we can watch our tensions disappear through the gift of his perfect grace. After all, the Lord Almighty is our release and relief from the tension of tidy.

Acknowledgments

AFTER PRAYING FOR years for the opportunity to work with a publisher, getting the fantastic news that the Lord paired me with Kregel Publications was unforgettable. Thank you to the entire Kregel team for making *The Tension of Tidy* a reality. Catherine, thank you for seeing the need for this book and appreciating my writing. Rachel, thank you for your wise leadership, your attention to detail, and the kind way you've shepherded me through this process. Moriah, it's been a joy to work with you. I've truly appreciated all your helpful recommendations and insight. Thank you, Tisha, for your grace-filled suggestions and guidance. Mark, Sarah, Jeane, Kayliani, Amy, and Lindsay, thank you!

My blog readers, it is such a gift of God to be part of your lives! Thank you for reading what I write, sharing your stories with me, and praying for me. I know you feel the tension of tidy. I do too! It's truly been my pleasure to dive into this struggle to help you.

I'm so grateful for my faithful sisters at The Chapel in Green. Thank you for your encouragement! Yiniva, Peggy, Nancy, Michele, Melissa, Mary, Logan, Linda, Kris, Kim, Jeanne, Jane, Jan, Jamie, Fran, Donnita, Cindy, Asheritah, Arieane, and Angie, your specific prayers have brought so much peace and clarity to my life and this book.

Thank you, Mike, Happy, Walt, and the staff at The Chapel in Green for your wise counsel, prayers, and teaching. You are my favorite coworkers and co-laborers. It's a gift to learn from you and a joy to serve with you!

Carmen, your prayers are vital. I'm so glad we've been able to watch the way the Lord has faithfully worked in our lives, writing, and ministries since our Girl with a Pearl and Accidentally Green days. You are a true friend, mentor, and my dearest big sister in Christ.

Keitha, I adore our talks, walks, and friendship. From homeschooling to theater to hanging out as families, I'm so thankful for you and the way you listen and help me process life and writing.

Kristy, you have an incredible gift of encouragement. I have no idea what I would do without you and your friendship. I thank God that he gave me a sister at *The Tan and Cardinal*. Thank you for your decades of listening to, understanding, and encouraging me!

Barb, I am so grateful to be represented by you and Books & Such. Thank you for working tirelessly, communicating clearly, teaching me how to become a better writer, and always having time to talk through details. Without your sage advice, this book wouldn't have been written.

Mary and Brian, I truly appreciate your continued encouragement and love. I'm thankful for both of you!

Mama and Daddy, thank you for reading to me since I was a baby and teaching me to read at such a young age. It means so much that you read all my homemade books, took me to Young Authors contests, mailed my queries and author fan letters, supported me through college and internships, and encouraged me to write. I'm so grateful God's blessed me with you, your love, and your prayers!

Eloise, no one else in this entire world is as amazing of a helper as you. Thank you for listening to me, speaking truth, and giving great advice. I love you!

Ezra, I've always been in awe of the way you communicate. Thank you for encouraging me, believing in me, and for spurring me on to be brave and obedient. I love you!

Aaron, you have been my biggest cheerleader, my most faithful encourager, and my best friend. The way you gently but persistently nudge me to keep writing and serving the Lord is exactly what I need. Thank you for doing so much extra so I can devote my time and energy to this life of ministry. I appreciate that you never grumble when I need to write and edit at night, on weekends, and until the wee hours of the morning. I love you, and I'm so glad that I get to spend my life with you.

Lord Jesus, you are the Word made flesh. Getting to use words to point others to you is such an honor, privilege, and gift. I'm so grateful for the way you continue to light my path and guide my way. Thank you for giving me words when I don't have any. Thank you for giving me clarity when life seems confusing. And thank you for filling me when it feels like I'm poured out and completely empty. Forever I am grateful for your rescue, mercy, and unending love. To you belong all praise, glory, wisdom, thanks, honor, power, and strength for ever and ever.

Notes

Chapter 1—Perfection
1. Lydia Brownback, *Sing a New Song: A Woman's Guide to the Psalms* (Crossway, 2017), 280.

Chapter 3—Peers
1. Genesis 25, 27; Judges 16; Numbers 13.
2. Melanie Dale, *Women Are Scary: The Totally Awkward Adventure of Finding Mom Friends* (HarperCollins Christian, 2015), 56–57.

Chapter 4—Family
1. Charles H. Spurgeon, *The Treasury of David* (Kregel, 1976), 213.

Chapter 5—Young Children
1. Kathleen D. Vohs, "It's Not 'Mess.' It's Creativity," *The New York Times*, September 13, 2013, https://www.nytimes.com/2013/09/15/opinion/sunday/its-not-mess-its-creativity.html.
2. Eleanor Barkhorn, "Messy Kids Learn More," *The Atlantic*, December 6, 2013, https://www.theatlantic.com/education/archive/2013/12/messy-kids-learn-more/282095/; National Institute of Heath, "It's a Kid's Job: Playing Helps Kids Learn and Grow," NIH News in Health, June 2012, https://newsinhealth.nih.gov/2012/06/its-kids-job.

3. Barry York, "The Pilgrim's Psalter," *Gentle Reformation*, September 8, 2014, https://gentlereformation.com/2014/09/08/the-pilgrims-psalter.

4. Eugene Peterson, *A Long Obedience in the Same Direction: Discipleship in an Instant Society* (InterVarsity, 2000), 11.

Chapter 7—Spouses

1. Sheila Wray Gregoire, *To Love, Honor, and Vacuum: When You Feel More Like a Maid Than a Wife and Mother* (Kregel, 2014), 43.

2. Rhea Grover, "Dirtiness Is Perceived by All, Cleanliness Is Pursued by Women," Harvard University, July 15, 2019, https://sitn.hms.harvard.edu/flash/2019/dirtiness-perceived-cleanliness-sustained-women-study-reveals.

3. Charles H. Spurgeon, *The Treasury of David* (Kregel, 1976), 595.

Chapter 10—Busyness

1. Kendra Adachi, *The Lazy Genius Way: Embrace What Matters, Ditch What Doesn't, and Get Stuff Done* (Penguin Random House, 2020), 116.

2. Becky Beresford, *She Believed HE Could, So She Did: Trading Culture's Lies for Christ-Centered Empowerment* (Moody, 2024), 32–33.

3. Emily P. Freeman, *The Next Right Thing: A Simple, Soulful Practice for Making Life Decisions* (Baker, 2019), 61.

Chapter 11—Too Much

1. Kait Hanson, "Marie Kondo Is Choosing Children over Organizing: 'I Realize What Is Important to Me,'" TODAY.com, January 27, 2023, https://www.today.com/parents/moms/marie-kondo-chooses-kids-over-cleaning-rcna67915#.

2. Joe Pinsker, "Why Are American Homes So Big?," *The Atlantic*, September 12, 2019, https://www.theatlantic.com/family/archive/2019/09/american-houses-big/597811.

3. "The American Family Today," Pew Research Center, Decem-

ber 17, 2015, https://www.pewresearch.org/social-trends/2015/12/17/1-the-american-family-today.

4. Colton Gardner, "Self Storage Industry Statistics (2022)," *Neighbor Blog*, Neighbor, May 6, 2022, https://www.neighbor.com/storage-blog/self-storage-industry-statistics.

5. Dana K. White, *Decluttering at the Speed of Life: Winning Your Never-Ending Battle with Stuff* (HarperCollins Christian, 2018).

6. "About the KonMari Method," KonMari, accessed March 13, 2024, https://konmari.com/about-the-konmari-method/.

7. Kyle Idleman, *Gods at War: Defeating the Idols that Battle for Your Heart* (HarperCollins Christian, 2018), 175.

8. Idleman, *Gods at War*, 30.

9. Dee Brestin, *The Jesus Who Surprises: Opening Our Eyes to His Presence in All of Life and Scripture* (Penguin Random House, 2019), 56.

10. Helen Howarth Lemmel, "Turn Your Eyes Upon Jesus," 1922, public domain.

Chapter 12—Discontentment

1. Elisabeth Elliot, *Keep a Quiet Heart* (Baker, 1995), 91.

2. Elliot, *Keep a Quiet Heart*, 91.

3. Brent Curtis and John Eldredge, *The Sacred Romance: Drawing Closer to the Heart of God* (Thomas Nelson, 1997), 20–21.

4. Max Lucado, *Traveling Light: Releasing the Burdens You Were Never Intended to Bear* (HarperCollins Christian, 2001), 153.

Chapter 14—You

1. Gary M. Landsberg and Sagi Denenberg, "Social Behavior of Sheep," *Merck Veterinary Manual*, May 2014, https://www.merckvetmanual.com/behavior/normal-social-behavior-and-behavioral-problems-of-domestic-animals/social-behavior-of-sheep.

2. Max Lucado, *Traveling Light: Releasing the Burdens You Were Never Intended to Bear* (HarperCollins Christian, 2001), 137.

About the Author

HILARY BERNSTEIN is the women's ministry director at The Chapel in Green in northeast Ohio, where she leads more than a thousand women closer to Christ and each other. An author, blogger, and former newspaper editor and columnist, Hilary has written more than a dozen devotional books. She helps women experience peace and purpose in their lives and homes through blog posts and weekly emails. A planner, foodie, and frequent hostess, Hilary loves to both travel and spend time at home with her husband, son, and daughter.

For more of Hilary's grace-filled, practical homemaking and home management tips and resources, visit www.hilarybernstein.com.